Flavor of
NEW ENGLAND

INTRODUCED BY JUDITH FERGUSON
FOOD PHOTOGRAPHY BY NEIL SUTHERLAND AND PETER BARRY
DESIGNED BY SALLY STRUGNELL AND ALISON JEWELL

2329
This edition produced for Book Express, Inc.
Airport Business Center
29 Kripes Road, East Granby, Connecticut, USA
© 1989 CLB Publishing Ltd., Godalming, Surrey, England
Printed and bound in Spain
All rights reserved
ISBN 1 85833 041 6

USA direct sales rights in this edition are exclusive to Book Express, Inc.

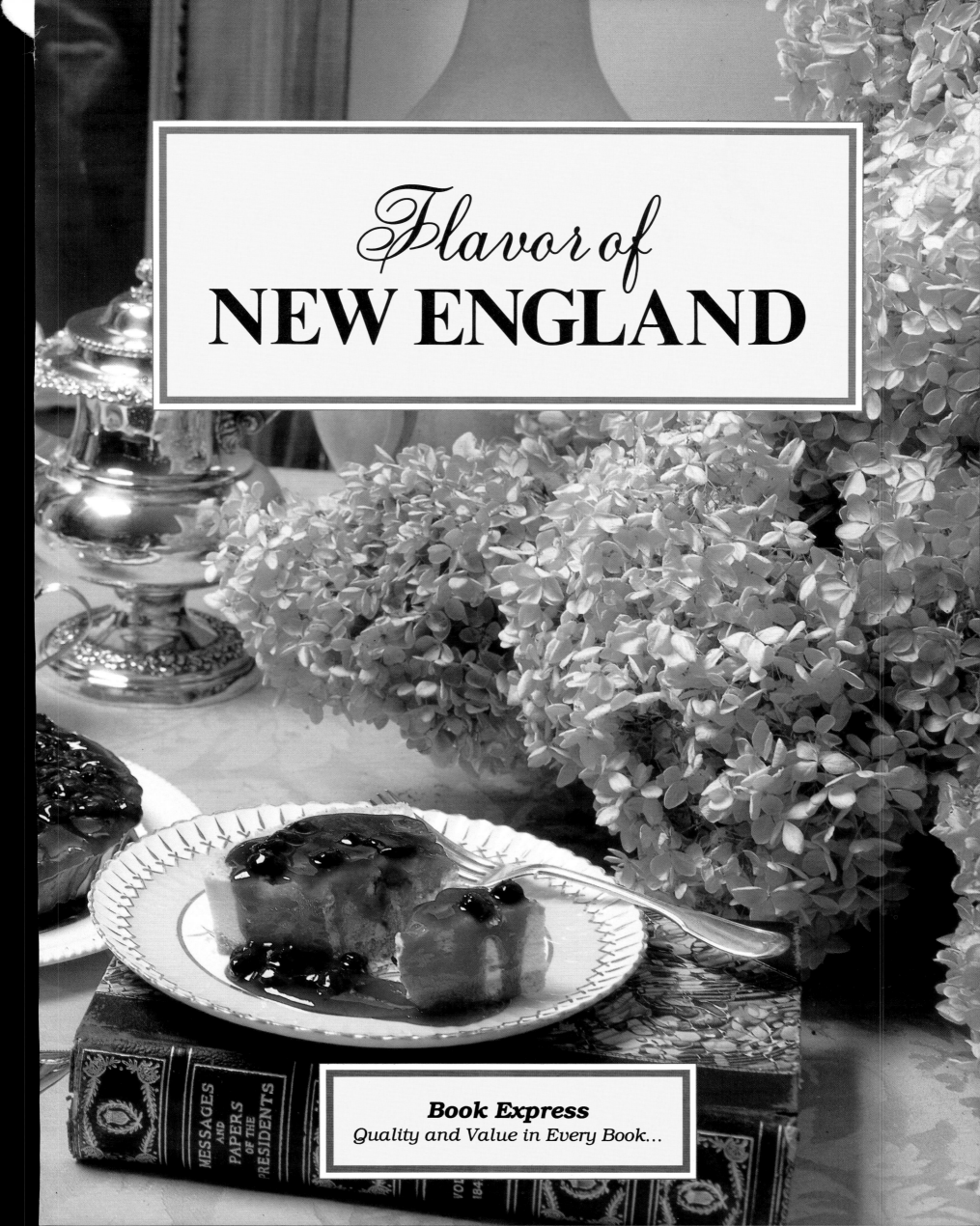

Flavor of
NEW ENGLAND

Book Express

Quality and Value in Every Book...

Contents

Picture shows Roast Prime Ribs of Beef Red Lion.
Chef Stephen Mongeon, The Red Lion Inn, Stockbridge, MA.

The history of a country isn't just about events, it's about people too; about their ideas, their occupations and preoccupations, their dress and, of course, their food. Many of today's New England states formed part of the original thirteen colonies and so are closely identified with the beginnings of the modern United States. It is to New England that we look to see the foods our forebears ate and this, together with the development of certain recipes through the years, can give us greater insight into the country's development as a whole. Some New England recipes, such as pumpkin pie and baked beans, give us a taste of history itself, as they have come down to us virtually unchanged since the days when our ancestors first enjoyed them.

The people who first settled the territory that became the New England states faced great hardships and near starvation in their first year. Their own crops having failed, they were forced to rely on native crops to survive, despite the unfamiliar and indeed exotic nature of these. It was the native Indians who introduced the settlers to maize, squash, tomatoes and pumpkins and to the wild turkeys they had domesticated. Cranberries were another gift from the Indians, who not only ate this indigenous fruit but used it for everything from a fabric dye to a poultice for arrow wounds. The berries soon went into traditional English recipes for pies and steamed puddings with great success. Maple syrup was unheard of in Europe but, although it must have seemed laughable to eat the sap of a tree, this delicacy soon made its own delicious contribution to the settlers' diet.

New England also provided a wealth of both wild game and, with its long sea coast, of seafood. The settlers were already familiar with oysters and mussels, but soon they were also eating clams of all sizes, in soups and chowders, with different stuffings or simply steamed. Lobsters were so plentiful that they were considered common fare and people would apologize if it was all they could offer their guests. Imagine that with today's lobster prices!

Influences on the cuisine of New England have been French, German and Italian, as well as English. In addition, each state has made its own individual contributions.

Connecticut was a farming state, so soup and side dish recipes using its vegetable produce were a natural culinary development. Meanwhile, some of New England's most elegant and exquisite food was served in the famous mansions of Rhode Island. Butterfish were so easy to catch off the state's long coastline that they became immensely popular, even for breakfast!

Massachusetts gave the country its first "fast food," Boston baked beans. With nowhere to stop for a meal for hundreds of miles, travelers had to carry their own food, so during the winter months baked beans would be wrapped in a cloth and left outside overnight to freeze. The next day they would be reheated over an open fire along the way.

Vermont is famous for its maple syrup, which combines so wonderfully with baked apples, squash and pumpkins or makes a heavenly mousse when folded into whipped cream. Vermont's thickly forested hills also provide lots of wild game, and many delicious recipes for using it.

New Hampshire's recipes may be traditional, but they're varied and ingenious, too, because its citizens are always ready to try new ways with old-fashioned dishes. So baked beans are combined with maple syrup and bourbon, and roast duck is given a tart cranberry glaze.

In Maine, lobster is king of the table. It is part of the famous New England shore dinner, a combination lobster and clambake. It also goes into creamy soups and stews or is baked and stuffed for an elegant main course. With all this delicious seafood, there doesn't seem room for dessert until you contemplate fresh strawberry shortcake or crisp meringues and cream.

Wherever you live, you would have to admit that New England has given us all a culinary heritage to be justly proud of.

Facing page: a tempting array of desserts photographed at Hammersmith Farm, Newport, Rhode Island. All recipes by Chef Peter T. Crowley, La Forge Casino Restaurant.

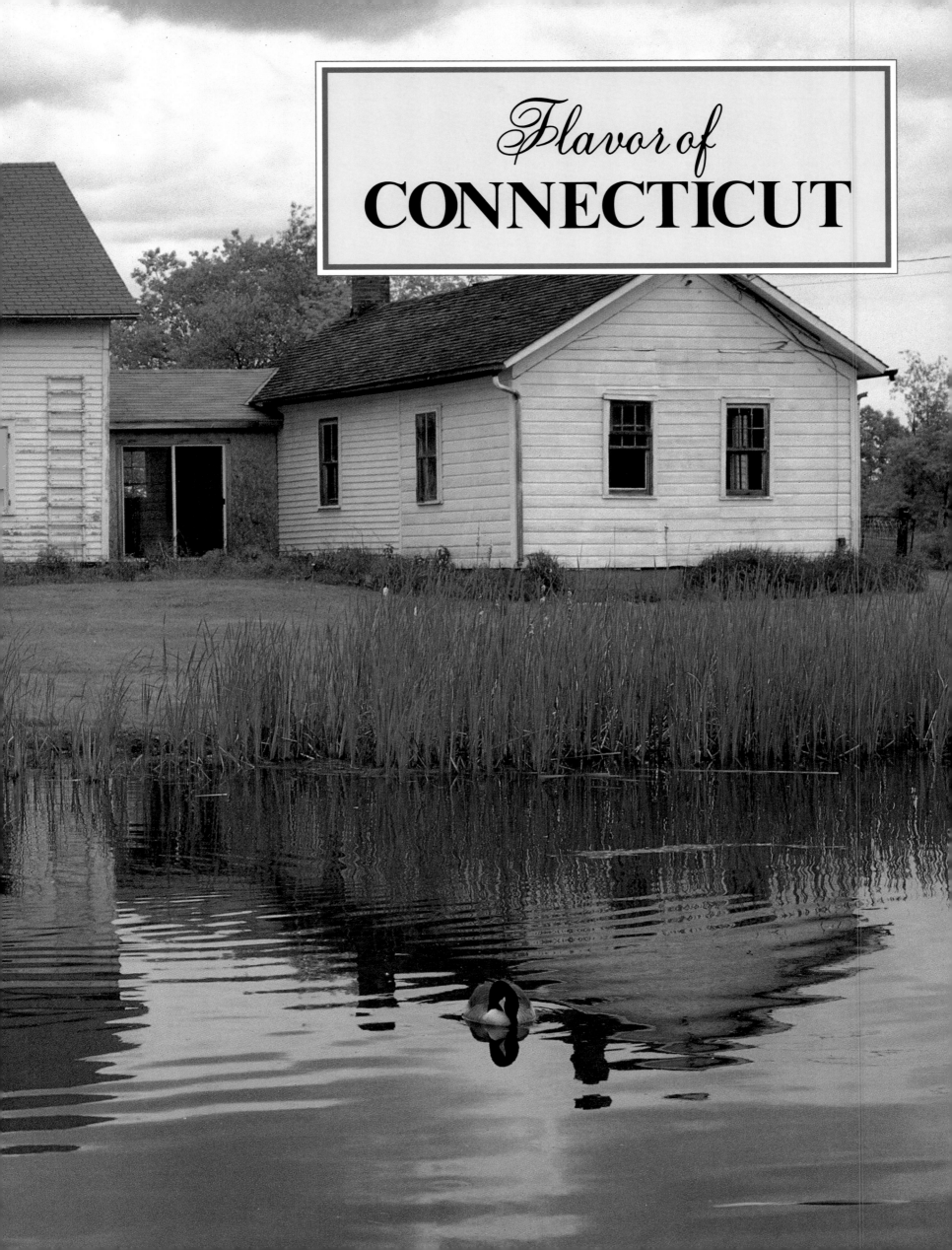

Flavor of
CONNECTICUT

BUTTERNUT SQUASH SOUP

This soup is traditional New England fare. The flesh of the butternut squash is denser and meatier than other varieties, so it makes a rich, thick soup without any additional thickening.

PREPARATION TIME: 25 minutes

COOKING TIME: 30-45 minutes

SERVES: 4-6

INGREDIENTS

☐ 1 butternut squash, peeled, seeds removed and cubed
☐ 1 onion, diced   ☐ 1 apple, peeled, cored and sliced
☐ 2 chicken bouillon cubes   ☐ 1½ cups milk
☐ 2 tbsps brown sugar   ☐ Pinch salt and pepper
☐ 2 tbsps butter

Place the prepared squash in a large pot with the apple and half the onion. Pour in the bouillon, cover the pot and cook until the squash is just tender. Do not overcook. Melt the butter in a sauté pan and cook the remaining onion until translucent and golden in color. Strain the soup and reserve the liquid. Place the squash, apple and onion in a food processor and return to the pot. Do not overwork the mixture; it should be coarsely chopped. Add 1½ cups milk to the soup and reheat gently. Add the sautéed onion and the sugar and enough of the reserved liquid to bring the soup to a thick, creamy consistency.

DANIEL ROUTHIER,
STONIHURST COTTAGE,
HIGHLAND FALLS
(FORMERLY OF STONINGTON, CT)

Previous pages: these geese and two goslings were photographed near Cornwall Bridge. Above: waterfalls are a common sight in Connecticut's rolling hills.
Facing page: this 19th-century whaling ship, the Charles W. Morgan, *is moored at Mystic Seaport.*

CABBAGE SOUP

This is a quickly prepared soup with a very traditional country flavor.

PREPARATION TIME: 20 minutes

COOKING TIME: 45 minutes

SERVES: 6

INGREDIENTS

□ 1 small cabbage, finely chopped   □ ½ a small onion, chopped
□ 2 carrots, peeled and grated
□ Beef stock or 3 rounded tsps beef bouillon powder or
3 bouillon cubes

Cook the cabbage, onion and carrots in the stock or bouillon with just enough water to cover. Cook about 45 minutes or until the vegetables are tender. Add salt and pepper to taste and serve.

MRS. MARY ROY,
STONIHURST COTTAGE,
HIGHLAND FALLS
(FORMERLY OF STONINGTON, CT)

Previous pages (clockwise from top): Butternut Squash Soup, Cabbage Soup and Pea Soup, photographed at the home of Arnold Copper, Stonington. Above: the area around the Charles Goodwin Dam near Colebrook.

PEA SOUP

Dried peas have been a staple food in this country since the first settlers set foot on dry land. Almost every country in the Western World has a recipe for pea soup, but the addition of a ham bone seems to be particularly American.

PREPARATION TIME: 20 minutes

COOKING TIME: 30-40 minutes

SERVES: 6-8

INGREDIENTS

- ☐ 1 package split green peas (no soaking required)
- ☐ 1 tbsp grated onion
- ☐ 1 stalk celery, thinly sliced
- ☐ 1 carrot, peeled and thinly sliced
- ☐ 1 ham bone with some meat attached

Pick over the split peas and add them to a large pot along with all the other ingredients. Cover with water and cook for 30-40 minutes, adding more water if needed. Remove the bone from the soup, take off the meat and chop it finely. Return the meat to the soup and serve with parsley and crackers.

MRS. MARY ROY,
STONIHURST COTTAGE,
HIGHLAND FALLS
(FORMERLY OF STONINGTON, CT)

Above: Mystic Seaport is a replica 19th-century seaport constructed on the site of the once-thriving shipyard of George Greenman and Co.

CORN PUDDING

Corn has been a valuable food throughout the history of this country. It was the corn crop that saved the Massachusetts Bay Colony and corn recipes found their way to Connecticut from there.

PREPARATION TIME: 20 minutes

COOKING TIME: 45 minutes

OVEN TEMPERATURE: 350°F

SERVES: 6-8

INGREDIENTS

☐ 2 cups Carnation milk or thin cream   ☐ 2 cups canned or fresh corn
☐ 2 tbsps melted butter   ☐ 2 tsps sugar
☐ 1 tsp salt   ☐ ¼ tsp pepper
☐ 3 eggs, well beaten

Add the milk, corn, butter, sugar and seasonings to the eggs. Pour into a well greased casserole and bake in a moderate oven for about 45 minutes or until the pudding is set. Insert a knife into the center of the pudding and if it comes out clean the pudding is done. For variety, add ¼ cup chopped green peppers or pimento, ½ cup minced ham or chopped mushrooms.

ISABELLA WITT,
STONIHURST COTTAGE,
HIGHLAND FALLS
(FORMERLY OF STONINGTON, CT)

Above: the Conestoga wagon is a reminder of the pioneering spirit of the state's first settlers.
Facing page: this fall landscape composition was taken near Willimantic.

GRILLED BLUEFISH WITH LIME-GINGER MARINADE

Here is yet another recipe for this popular fish, but this time in an oriental style. Besides adding flavor to this fish, the marinade helps to keep it moist while grilling.

PREPARATION TIME: 15 minutes plus 3 hours chilling
COOKING TIME: 8-10 minutes
SERVES: 2

INGREDIENTS

☐ 2 large bluefish fillets, with skin

MARINADE

☐ ½ cup fresh lime juice   ☐ 1 tsp grated lime rind
☐ 3 cloves garlic, crushed   ☐ ½ cup olive oil
☐ 2 tsps minced fresh ginger   ☐ Salt and pepper

Mix the marinade ingredients together and pour over the bluefish fillets in a shallow dish. Turn to coat both sides well and cover. Marinate for 3 hours in the refrigerator. On hot charcoal or in a preheated gas grill, cook the flesh side of the fillet first for approximately 5 minutes or until the fish is lightly browned. Turn over and baste the fish well with the marinade. Grill the skin side an additional 3 to 5 minutes or until the fish is thoroughly cooked. Reheat the marinade and transfer the fish to a hot serving platter. Pour the remaining marinade over the fish to serve. This marinade is good with other oily fish such as tuna or salmon.

DANIEL ROUTHIER,
STONIHURST COTTAGE,
HIGHLAND FALLS
(FORMERLY OF STONINGTON, CT)

BAKED WHOLE BLUEFISH

This is an impressive way to serve this popular New England fish for a dinner party. The colorful garnish dresses it up and gives extra flavor.

PREPARATION TIME: 30 minutes

COOKING TIME: 1 hour 15 minutes

OVEN TEMPERATURE: 250°F

SERVES: 4

INGREDIENTS

- 1 bluefish, 18–20 inches long
- 2 lemons
- ¾ cup white wine or vermouth
- ½ cup olive oil
- ¼ lb butter
- ¼ cup water
- Ground black pepper
- 1 large red onion, chopped
- Fresh chives, sage, thyme, oregano, dill and parsley
- ½ cup shrimp (optional)
- 4 scallops (optional)
- 1 cup small whole mushrooms
- ¼ lb whole cherry tomatoes, stems removed

GARNISH

- Lemon wedges
- Parsley sprigs
- Dill sprigs
- Whole cherry tomatoes

Thoroughly grease a large, shallow baking pan with the olive oil and place in the fish, head and tail on. Stuff the belly of the fish with whole fresh herbs and chopped onion. Pour the olive oil over the fish and sprinkle with chopped herbs and a pinch of pepper and salt. Dot with butter and pour over the juice of two lemons, wine and water. Place in a preheated oven and baste occasionally while cooking for 1 hour. Remove the dish from the oven and add the shrimp and scallops, if using. Also add the mushrooms and cherry tomatoes. Replace in the oven and cook for 10-15 minutes more. Allow the fish to stand in the cooking liquid for 15 minutes then remove to a warm platter for serving. Place the shrimp, scallops, tomatoes and mushrooms around the fish with the lemon wedges, sprigs or parsley, dill and additional tomatoes.

ARNOLD COPPER,
MADISON AVENUE,
NEW YORK CITY,
AND STONINGTON, CT

Previous pages: Baked Whole Bluefish, photographed at the home of Arnold Copper, Stonington.
Facing page: the family dog keeps an eye out for visitors to this charming old house in Chester.

SKEWERED SEAFOOD AND PORK WITH LIME-CURRY MARINADE

These fish kabobs can be cooked under a preheated gas grill or over hot coals. The combination of fish and pork with a lime and curry marinade gives this barbecue food an Indonesian flavor.

PREPARATION TIME: 25 minutes

COOKING TIME: 8-10 minutes

SERVES: 4

INGREDIENTS

- □ 8 large sea scallops □ 8 large shrimp, shelled, leaving the end of the tail on if desired
- □ ½ lb thick sliced roast pork □ ¼ lb snow peas
- □ 1 mango, peeled and cut into chunks
- □ 1 fresh pineapple, peeled and cut into chunks
- □ Red plums, halved and stoned

MARINADE

- □ ½ cup olive oil □ 1 tbsp curry powder (or to taste)
- □ ½ cup fresh lime juice

Make sure the vein running along the back of the shrimp is removed and also any tough muscle attached to the sea scallops. If the plums are large, cut them into quarters. Break off the stems of the snow peas and pull backwards to remove the stringy fibers.

Place the ingredients on the skewers in the following manner: pork with pineapple and plum, alternating the ingredients, shrimp with snow peas, scallops with mango. Use separate skewers for any leftover peas or fruit. Mix the marinade ingredients and brush over the prepared skewers. Grill over hot coals or on a preheated grill for 8-10 minutes, basting frequently. Do not have the racks too close to the coals and remember that the scallops and shrimp will cook a bit faster than the pork. Serve the skewers over rice.

DANIEL ROUTHIER,
STONIHURST COTTAGE,
HIGHLAND FALLS
(FORMERLY OF STONINGTON, CT)

Facing page: Skewered Seafood and Pork with Lime-Curry Marinade, photographed at the home of Arnold Copper, Stonington.

BOILED NEW ENGLAND DINNER

This has been a continual favorite in the New England states and across the country. The parsnips are a delicious idea as a substitute for the turnips which traditionally appear. It wasn't until the 1730s that potatoes were included.

PREPARATION TIME: 30 minutes

COOKING TIME: 3-3½ hours

SERVES: 8

INGREDIENTS

☐ 4lbs corned beef brisket ☐ 8 medium-sized potatoes
☐ 6-8 carrots, peeled ☐ 1 head cabbage
☐ 6-8 small parsnips, peeled

Rinse the corned beef and cook for 3-3½ hours, covered with water. Slice the vegetables, add them to the beef and cook until tender. Season with salt and pepper and serve sprinkled with chopped parsley.

MRS. MARY ROY,
STONIHURST COTTAGE,
HIGHLAND FALLS
(FORMERLY OF STONINGTON, CT)

Above: Boiled New England Dinner, photographed outside the home of Arnold Copper, Stonington.

RED FLANNEL HASH

The name comes from the color of the dish, made bright with the addition of cooked beets. It frequently features on brunch menus.

PREPARATION TIME: 20 minutes

COOKING TIME: 25-30 minutes

SERVES: 4

INGREDIENTS

- 1lb cold corned beef
- 3-4 cold boiled potatoes, roughly chopped
- 1 medium onion, finely chopped
- Salt, pepper and nutmeg
- 1-2 cooked beets, peeled and diced
- 2 tbsps butter or bacon fat

Cut the meat into small pieces. If using a food processor, be careful not to overwork. Combine all the remaining ingredients except the butter or bacon fat. Melt the butter or fat in a frying pan and, when foaming, place in the mixture. Spread it out evenly in the pan. Cook over low heat, pressing the mixture down continuously with a wooden spoon or spatula. Cook about 15-20 minutes. When a crust forms on the bottom, turn over and brown the other side. Cut into wedges and remove from the pan to serve.

Above: Red Flannel Hash makes a perfect brunch dish with the addition of a poached egg.

JOHNNYCAKES

Indians made their corn bread by grinding corn, mixing it with water and baking it in a cake-like patty over a hot fire. These were known as Journey Cakes because they were easy to prepare when traveling, and somehow came to be called Johnnycakes.

PREPARATION TIME: 10 minutes

COOKING TIME: 11 minutes

MAKES: 8-10 cakes

INGREDIENTS

- ☐ 1 cup cornmeal
- ☐ 1¼ cups water
- ☐ 1 tsp salt
- ☐ 1 tsp sugar

Mix the cornmeal and salt and sugar together. Boil the water and beat in gradually until the batter is smooth, but very thick (it may not be necessary to add all the water). Drop onto a well greased, hot griddle and fry over medium heat for 6 minutes. Turn over and cook on the other side for 5 minutes. Serve immediately.

Above: light and airy, White Memdhal Farm is set in beautiful gardens near Litchfield.

PUMPKIN RAISIN NUT BREAD

Raisins and nuts make a nice addition to this spicy bread. Try serving it and the plain pumpkin bread slightly warm, spread with butter or cream cheese.

PREPARATION TIME: 20 minutes
COOKING TIME: 1 hour
OVEN TEMPERATURE: 350°F
MAKES: 2 loaves

INGREDIENTS

- 1 cup vegetable oil
- 4 eggs, beaten
- ⅔ cup water
- 2 cups canned or fresh pumpkin
- 3½ cups sifted flour
- 1½ tsps salt
- 1 tsp ground cloves
- 2 tsps baking soda
- ½ tsp baking powder
- 1 tsp nutmeg
- 1 tsp cinnamon
- 2⅔ cups sugar
- 1 cup raisins
- 1 cup chopped pecans

Grease and flour the loaf pans and set them aside. Combine the oil, eggs, water and pumpkin. Sift in the dry ingredients and blend until moistened. Stir in the raisins and pecans and divide the mixture between the two pans. Bake 1 hour in a preheated oven, or until a knife inserted into the center of the bread comes out clean.

MRS. RITA ROUTHIER,
STONIHURST COTTAGE,
HIGHLAND FALLS
(FORMERLY OF STONINGTON, CT)

Above: the church at Old Mystic Village, a reconstruction of an old colonial settlement.

PUMPKIN BREAD

The addition of pumpkin in this quick bread recipe makes for a very moist bread with a beautiful color.

PREPARATION TIME: 20 minutes
COOKING TIME: 1 hour
OVEN TEMPERATURE: 350°F
MAKES: 1 9″ x 5″ loaf

—————— INGREDIENTS ——————

☐ 1 cup canned pumpkin   ☐ 2 eggs
☐ 2 cups flour   ☐ ¾ cup sugar
☐ ¼ tsp cinnamon   ☐ ¼ tsp nutmeg
☐ ⅛ tsp ground cloves   ☐ 1 tsp baking soda

Mix the pumpkin and the eggs together well and sift in the dry ingredients. Fold together and put into a well greased loaf pan. Bake 1 hour until a knife inserted into the center of the bread comes out clean.

ANNETTE MINER,
CIDER MILL,
STONINGTON, CT

Previous pages: Pumpkin Raisin-Nut Bread and Pumpkin Bread, Indian Pudding and Johnnycakes, photographed at the home of Arnold Copper, Stonington.
Above: water lilies prosper in the still waters of this pond near Old Mystic Village.

INDIAN PUDDING

The preparation of this pudding cannot be hurried. Cornmeal must thicken slowly and absorb the milk gradually or it will be hard and granular and the pudding will be spoiled. The traditional Indian version was, of course, much simpler, but the addition of apples, raisins and nuts makes this pudding fit for company.

PREPARATION TIME: 25 minutes

COOKING TIME: 55 minutes

OVEN TEMPERATURE: 350°F

SERVES: 8

INGREDIENTS

☐ 5 cups milk ☐ ½ cup cornmeal
☐ 1 cup dark molasses ☐ ¼ cup butter
☐ 1 tsp salt ☐ 2 eggs, well beaten
☐ 1 cup apples, cored and diced ☐ ½ cup raisins
☐ ½ cup chopped walnuts ☐ ½ tsp cinnamon

Bring the milk to the boil and slowly add the cornmeal, stirring constantly. Cook over very gentle heat or in the top part of a double boiler for about 25 minutes or until the cornmeal thickens. Add the molasses and the remaining ingredients. Pour into a well greased round baking dish. Bake for about 30 minutes. Serve warm with whipped cream or vanilla ice cream.

MRS. LINDA ROUTHIER,
STONIHURST COTTAGE,
HIGHLAND FALLS
(FORMERLY OF STONINGTON, CT)

Above: the magnificent State Capitol building in Hartford.

CRISP CRUSTY
WAFFLES

Waffles date from the beginning of the 19th century in the United States. Early waffle irons were put on top of the stove and even over an open flame, but they had to be turned at least once during cooking. When electric waffle irons were invented, waffles became even more popular. In addition to breakfast, waffles are often served for lunch or for a light supper. You can top them with butter and syrup or honey, creamed chicken or seafood, ham or bacon, or with fruit and ice cream or whipped cream for dessert.

PREPARATION TIME: 20 minutes
COOKING TIME: 5 minutes per waffle
MAKES: 6-7 waffles

INGREDIENTS

☐ 2 cups flour   ☐ 4 tsps baking powder
☐ 1 tsp salt   ☐ 3 eggs, separated
☐ 1¾ cups milk   ☐ ½ cup salad oil
☐ Pinch sugar

Sift together the flour, salt and baking powder. Beat the egg whites until stiff. Beat the yolks until light and add milk and oil. Stir the yolk and flour mixture together and fold in the egg whites. Heat the waffle iron and grease well. Spoon some of the mixture into the waffle iron and lower the lid. Take care not to put in too much batter as it will spread. Bake until the steam has stopped coming from around the edge of the iron and lift the lid to see if the waffle is nicely browned. If not, lower the lid and continue cooking for another minute or two until crisp.

MRS. RITA ROUTHIER,
STONIHURST COTTAGE,
HIGHLAND FALLS
(FORMERLY OF STONINGTON, CT)

Facing page: Blueberry Muffins and Crisp Crusty Waffles, photographed at the home of Arnold Copper, Stonington.

BLUEBERRY MUFFINS

Blueberries grow in abundance in the New England states and all over the country as well. Wild blueberries ripen in July, August and September and are a real treat to look forward to. Serve these light, tender muffins piping hot.

PREPARATION TIME: 20 minutes

COOKING TIME: 20 minutes

OVEN TEMPERATURE: 400°F

MAKES: 12 muffins

INGREDIENTS

☐ 1½ cups flour ☐ ½ cup sugar
☐ ¼ tsp salt ☐ 2 tsps baking powder
☐ 1 egg ☐ ¼ cup oil
☐ ½ cup milk ☐ 1 cup blueberries

Mix the flour, sugar, salt and baking powder and set aside. Mix the egg and oil until well blended. Add the wet ingredients to the dry ingredients, stirring in gradually. Fold in the blueberries and pour the batter into greased and floured muffin pans or pans lined with cupcake papers. Half-fill each hole in the pan. Bake for 20 minutes, or until well risen and nicely browned.

MRS. MARY ROY,
STONIHURST COTTAGE,
HIGHLAND FALLS
(FORMERLY OF STONINGTON, CT)

Above: an isolated farmstead at Newgate. Facing page: looking out over the rooftops of Yale University to the town of New Haven beyond.

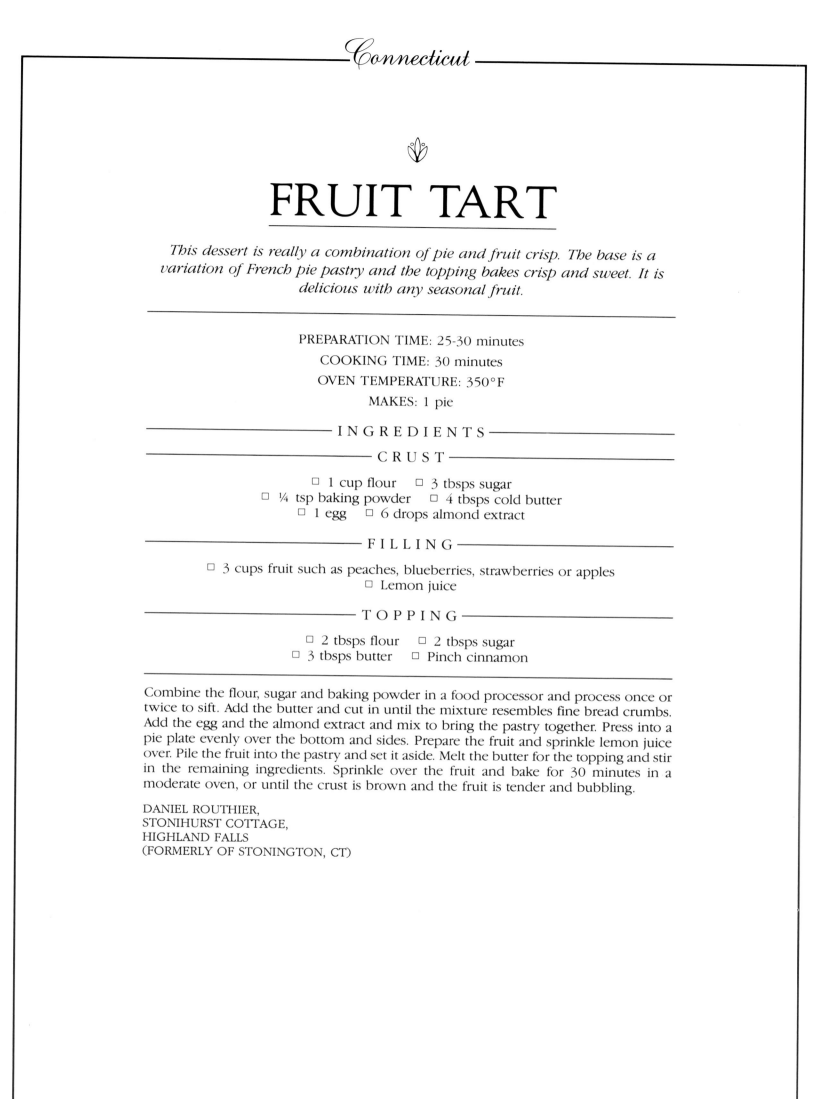

FRUIT TART

This dessert is really a combination of pie and fruit crisp. The base is a variation of French pie pastry and the topping bakes crisp and sweet. It is delicious with any seasonal fruit.

PREPARATION TIME: 25-30 minutes

COOKING TIME: 30 minutes

OVEN TEMPERATURE: 350°F

MAKES: 1 pie

INGREDIENTS

CRUST

☐ 1 cup flour   ☐ 3 tbsps sugar
☐ ¼ tsp baking powder   ☐ 4 tbsps cold butter
☐ 1 egg   ☐ 6 drops almond extract

FILLING

☐ 3 cups fruit such as peaches, blueberries, strawberries or apples
☐ Lemon juice

TOPPING

☐ 2 tbsps flour   ☐ 2 tbsps sugar
☐ 3 tbsps butter   ☐ Pinch cinnamon

Combine the flour, sugar and baking powder in a food processor and process once or twice to sift. Add the butter and cut in until the mixture resembles fine bread crumbs. Add the egg and the almond extract and mix to bring the pastry together. Press into a pie plate evenly over the bottom and sides. Prepare the fruit and sprinkle lemon juice over. Pile the fruit into the pastry and set it aside. Melt the butter for the topping and stir in the remaining ingredients. Sprinkle over the fruit and bake for 30 minutes in a moderate oven, or until the crust is brown and the fruit is tender and bubbling.

DANIEL ROUTHIER,
STONIHURST COTTAGE,
HIGHLAND FALLS
(FORMERLY OF STONINGTON, CT)

Facing page: Fruit Tart, photographed at the home of Arnold Copper, Stonington.

GINGERSNAPS

These have always been a favorite in American cookie jars. They were long considered a roll cookie, which meant that the dough was formed into a long sausage shape, chilled until firm and sliced. Now the dough can be shaped into balls or simply dropped on the greased baking sheets. Crushed and mixed with butter and sugar, they make a nice change from the usual graham cracker crust for pies or cheesecake.

PREPARATION TIME: 25 minutes
COOKING TIME: 12-15 minutes per batch
OVEN TEMPERATURE: 250°F
MAKES: 3 dozen cookies

———————————— INGREDIENTS ————————————

- 2 cups flour
- 2 tsps baking soda
- 1 tsp cinnamon
- ½ tsp salt
- ½ tsp ginger
- ¼ tsp ground cloves
- ¾ cup shortening
- 1 cup sugar
- 1 egg, well beaten
- ¼ cup molasses

Sift the dry ingredients together and set them aside. In a separate bowl, beat the shortening until light and gradually add the sugar. Beat in the eggs and molasses and then put in the dry ingredients. Form the dough into 1 inch balls and place them about 2 inches apart on greased cookie sheets. Flatten them with a fork and bake 12-15 minutes or until crisp. Allow to cool on the cookie sheet for 1 minute before transferring to a cooling rack. If the dough is too soft to shape, drop by teaspoonfuls onto the cookie sheets or refrigerate the dough until firm.

MRS. RITA ROUTHIER,
STONIHURST COTTAGE,
HIGHLAND FALLS
(FORMERLY OF STONINGTON, CT)

Facing page: built in 1801, Miles Lewis House in Bristol houses the American Clock and Watch Museum.

CHOCOLATE CHIP
COOKIES

Everyone has a slightly different version of this popular cookie. Long before chocolate was sold in small morsels, cooks had to cut up bars of chocolate into small chips, hence the name. These cookies were also known as Tollhouse Cookies, after the Tollhouse Restaurant, where the owner, Ruth Wakefield made these cookies popular.

PREPARATION TIME: 20 minutes

COOKING TIME: 10-12 minutes per batch

OVEN TEMPERATURE: 375°F

MAKES: approximately 3 dozen

INGREDIENTS

- ☐ 1 cup flour
- ☐ ½ tsp baking soda
- ☐ ½ tsp salt
- ☐ ½ cup shortening
- ☐ ½ cup sugar
- ☐ ¼ cup firmly packed brown sugar
- ☐ 1 egg
- ☐ 1 6oz package chocolate bits
- ☐ 1 tsp vanilla
- ☐ ½ cup nut meats

Put the flour, baking soda and salt into a bowl. Cream the shortening in a separate bowl and add the sugar gradually, creaming together until light and fluffy. Add the egg and beat in thoroughly. Add the dry ingredients in two parts and mix well. Finally stir in the chocolate bits, nuts and vanilla and mix well. Drop from a teaspoon, about 2 inches apart, onto ungreased baking sheets. Bake 10-12 minutes or until crisp. Allow to cool 1 minute on the baking sheet and remove to a cooling rack.

MRS. RITA ROUTHIER,
STONIHURST COTTAGE,
HIGHLAND FALLS
(FORMERLY OF STONINGTON, CT)

✿

AUNT HELEN'S CREAM CHEESECAKE

Cheesecake is one of the most popular desserts in the United States. This one makes use of New England's delicious blueberries in a sauce that complements the cake's velvety richness.

PREPARATION TIME: 30 minutes
COOKING TIME: 1 hour 10 minutes
MAKES: 1 cake

INGREDIENTS

CRUST

☐ 2 cups zwieback crumbs   ☐ ½ cup granulated sugar
☐ ½ cup melted, unsalted butter

FILLING

☐ 1½ lbs softened cream cheese   ☐ 2 tsps vanilla extract
☐ 1 cup granulated sugar   ☐ 5 eggs

TOPPING

☐ 1 quart sour cream   ☐ ¼ cup granulated sugar
☐ 2 tsps vanilla extract

BLUEBERRY SAUCE

☐ 1 cup granulated sugar   ☐ 2 tsps cornstarch
☐ ¼ tsp ground nutmeg   ☐ Pinch salt   ☐ 1 cup cold water
☐ 2½ cups fresh blueberries, picked over and cleaned,
or 4 cups frozen blueberries
☐ 3 tsps lemon juice

Combine the crust ingredients together and press into a 10″ spring pan. Press the mixture 2 inches up the sides of the pan and cover the bottom completely. Blend the filling ingredients together using a mixer or food processor, adding the eggs one at a time. Pour into the prepared crust and bake at 325°F for 1 hour. Remove the cake from the oven and let stand for 5 minutes. Mix the topping ingredients together and pour over the cake. Return the cake to the oven, raise the temperature to 375°F and bake for 8 minutes. Remove the cake from the oven and allow to cool on a rack at room temperature. Cover and chill thoroughly in the refrigerator, preferably overnight. Serve cut into 12 to 16 portions. To prepare the blueberry sauce, combine all the ingredients except the blueberries and lemon juice and cook over medium heat in a stainless steel pan. Stir constantly until the mixture thickens and comes to the boil. Cook about 2 minutes or until the mixture clears. Add the blueberries and return to the boil. Remove from the heat and immediately add the lemon juice. Add more lemon juice if necessary to adjust the sweetness. Serve a spoonful of sauce over or around the cheesecake slices.

NOAH'S RESTAURANT OF STONINGTON, CT

Facing page: photographed at the home of Arnold Copper, Stonington, Aunt Helen's Cream Cheesecake brings a Connecticut dinner party to a mouthwatering conclusion. Also featured are Gingersnaps and Chocolate Chip Cookies.

APPLE CRISP

Apple crisp is an old-fashioned dessert that has remained immensely popular over the years. Perhaps this is because it is so easy to make and so good to eat. The topping mixture can be made ahead of time and stored in the refrigerator to be used whenever the desire for apple crisp strikes.

PREPARATION TIME: 25 minutes
COOKING TIME: 45 minutes
OVEN TEMPERATURE: 350°F
SERVES: 4-6

INGREDIENTS

☐ 6-8 tart apples   ☐ ½ cup granulated sugar
☐ ¼ tsp ground cloves   ☐ ½ tsp cinnamon
☐ 2 tsps lemon juice

TOPPING

☐ ¾ cup flour   ☐ 6 tbsps butter
☐ ½ cup brown sugar

Peel and slice the apples. Blend the remaining ingredients and toss with the apples to mix thoroughly. Pour into a buttered 1½ quart casserole. Blend the topping ingredients together into a crumbly consistency and sprinkle over the top of the apples. Bake 45 minutes or until the apples are tender and the top is brown and crisp. Serve with cream or vanilla ice cream.

MARGARETHE Z. THOMAS
STONINGTON, CT

Above: the surroundings of Andersons Pond, North Stonington, are perfectly reflected in its still waters.

CIDER MILL APPLE DESSERT

This is a type of apple crisp and is a delicious way to use very tart apples.
The topping contains 1 whole cup of brown sugar
which cooks to a caramel crispness.

PREPARATION TIME: 25 minutes
COOKING TIME: 30 minutes
OVEN TEMPERATURE: 350°F
MAKES: 1 9″ dessert

INGREDIENTS

- □ 4 cups sliced apples
- □ ½ cup water
- □ 1 cup flour
- □ 1 cup light brown sugar
- □ 1 tsp cinnamon
- □ ½ cup butter, cut into small pieces

Peel the apples and slice them thinly into a 9-inch-round pie dish. Pour over the water and then mix the remaining ingredients until the pieces are the size of small peas. Spread the topping over the apples and bake until the apples are tender and the crust is brown and crisp, about 30 minutes.

ANNETTE MINER,
CIDER MILL,
STONINGTON, CT

Above: beyond this entrance lies the 19th century, as preserved at Mystic Seaport.

APPLE BUTTER

*Making a thick spread from very ripe fruit such as apples, plums or peaches
is an old Colonial culinary art. If no sugar or honey was available,
the fruit furnished the sweetness all on its own. Butters were
often cooked over open fires in the back yard in large copper
kettles and constantly stirred with long wooden paddles.*

PREPARATION TIME: 1 hour

COOKING TIME: 2-3 hours

MAKES: approximately 6 pints

INGREDIENTS

□ 10lbs tart red apples (approximately ½ bushel)
□ 1 tsp whole allspice   □ 1 tsp whole cloves
□ 2-3 sticks cinnamon   □ 2 sliced lemons or limes
□ 2 quarts apple cider   □ 2 cups granulated sugar

Wash, core and slice the apples but do not peel them. Place in a large, deep, heavy-based
pan with the spices and lemons or limes. Add boiling water to almost cover, and cook
slowly, uncovered, until the apples are slushy in consistency. This takes approximately
1 hour. If the cinnamon sticks have not softened, remove them from the mixture and
purée in a food processor or food mill. Rinse out the pot and add the apple cider. Bring
to the boil and stir in the sugar. After the sugar dissolves, add the apple purée and reduce
the heat. Cook over very low heat, stirring occasionally, but do not scrape the bottom.
Continue cooking slowly until the apple butter is ready to spread. To test it, spread a
tablespoon of the mixture on a piece of frozen bread. If it sets immediately, the apple
butter is done. Pour the hot apple butter into sterilized jars, seal and store.

PAUL MULLINS,
DEAN'S MILL FARM,
STONINGTON, CT

*Facing page: an array of tempting treats made from the best of the local apple crop: Baked Apples, Cider
Mill Apple Dessert, Apple Crisp and Apple Butter, all photographed outside the Cider Mill, Stonington.*

BAKED APPLES

Baked apples are a comforting, warming dessert that has long been popular in the United States. Sugar, cinnamon and raisins form the classic filling for baked apples, but the addition of slivered almonds and sherry make this version a bit special.

PREPARATION TIME: 20 minutes

COOKING TIME: 30-40 minutes

OVEN TEMPERATURE: 350°F

SERVES: 4

INGREDIENTS

□ 4 large, tart apples □ ½ cup brown sugar
□ 2 tbsps raisins □ 1 tsp cinnamon
□ ½ cup slivered almonds □ 1 cup water
□ 3 tbsps sherry

Core the apples, leaving half an inch at the bottom. Mix the filling ingredients together and fill the apples with the mixture. Place them in a shallow baking dish and add the water and sherry. Bake 30-40 minutes, until soft but not mushy. Serve with ice cream and spoon over the cooking liquid.

MARGARETHE Z. THOMAS
STONINGTON, CT

Above: an empty wooden building in Devil's Hopyard State Park.
Facing page: Wadsworth Falls form a dramatic backdrop for two fishermen in the State Park of the same name.

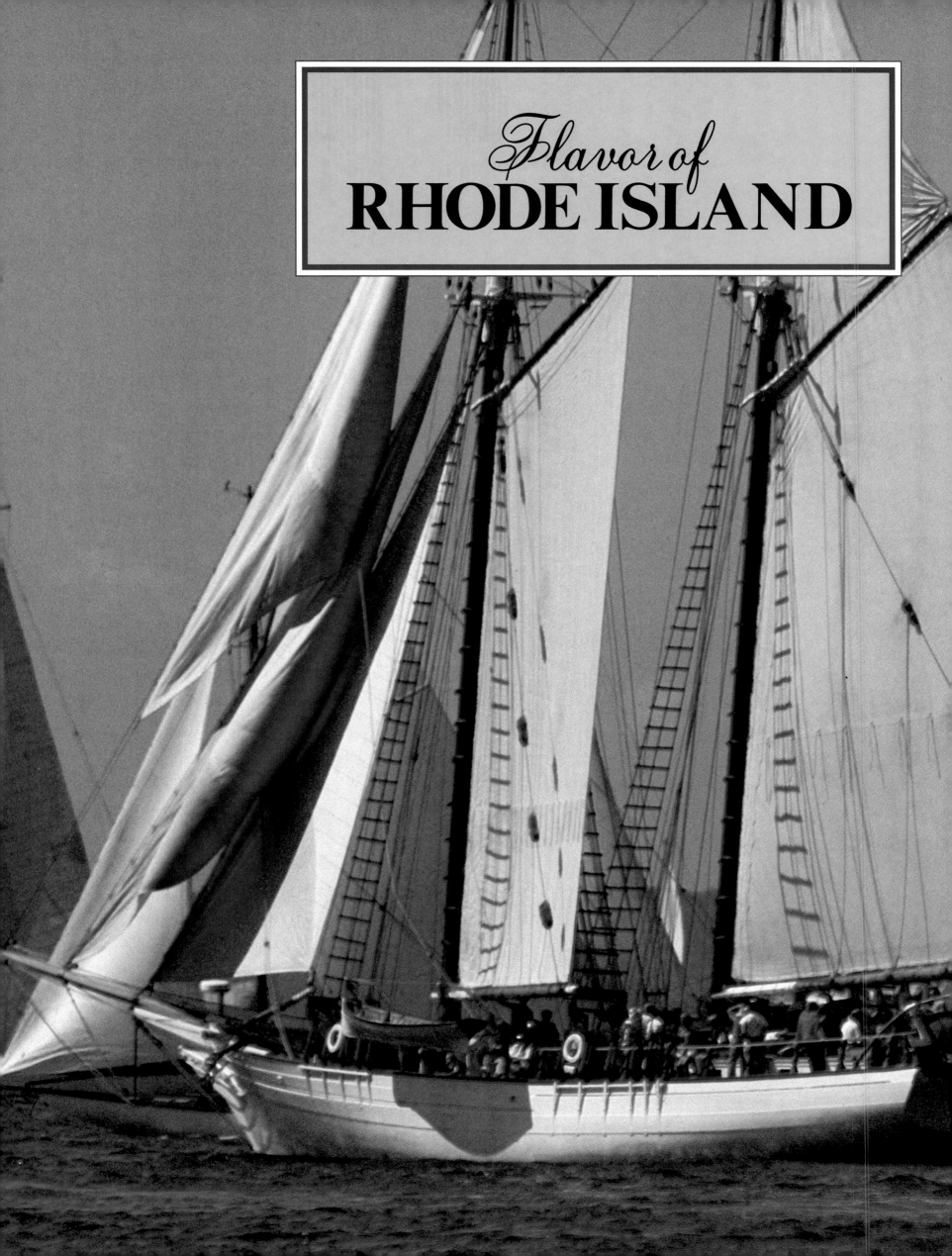

Flavor of
RHODE ISLAND

STEAMED MUSSELS

Inexpensive and quick to cook, mussels make an excellent first course. With olive oil, basil and Italian tomatoes in the ingredients, this seafood recipe shows the Italian influence that is so strong in parts of Rhode Island.

PREPARATION TIME: 25 minutes

COOKING TIME: 5 minutes

SERVES: 2

—————— I N G R E D I E N T S ——————

☐ 24 medium mussels, washed and debearded
☐ 1 rounded tsp chopped garlic   ☐ 2 tbsps olive oil
☐ Rosemary, oregano and basil to taste   ☐ 3oz dry white wine
☐ 3 chopped Italian tomatoes

Cook the garlic in the olive oil without browning. Add the herbs and white wine and boil well to reduce slightly. Add the tomatoes and mussels, cover and steam until the mussels open (about 5 minutes). Discard any musssels that do not open. Serve with chunks of toasted French bread.

THE OLYMPIA TEA ROOM,
BAY STREET, WATCH HILL, RI

*Above: Steamed Mussels and (foreground) Stuffed Quahogs,
photographed at Steven Mack's Chase Hill Farm, coastal Rhode Island.*

STUFFED QUAHOGS

Quahogs are hard-shell clams that are used for chowder when large, and eaten on the half shell when smaller. To facilitate opening, place well-scrubbed clams in a pan in a moderate oven and heat until they open. Use a strong knife to pry off the top shells. One or two stuffed clams make an excellent hors d'oeuvre or appetizer, more make a great snack or meal. One clam stuffs one shell.

PREPARATION TIME: 20 minutes

COOKING TIME: 15 minutes

OVEN TEMPERATURE: 375°F

SERVES: 4

———— I N G R E D I E N T S ————

☐ 8 quahogs, shelled, poached 3 minutes and chopped
☐ 1 onion, chopped   ☐ ¼ tsp oregano
☐ 1 green and 1 red pepper, chopped   ☐ 1 clove garlic, crushed
☐ 3 tbsps butter   ☐ Fresh bread crumbs
☐ Grated Romano or Parmesan cheese

Sauté the onions and peppers in butter until glassy, add the chopped garlic and cook another 1-2 minutes over low heat. Stir in the chopped clams and an equal amount of fresh bread crumbs. Add about ½ tsp grated cheese per clam. Moisten with additional melted butter and/or clam juice. Stuff into each clam shell half and bake until hot and slightly browned. Serve accompanied with lemon wedges and hot pepper sauce (Tabasco).

THE OLYMPIA TEA ROOM,
BAY STREET, WATCH HILL, RI

Above: Providence's imposing Capitol is built of white Georgia marble and topped by a symbolic bronze statue of The Independent Man.

RHODE ISLAND
CLAM CHOWDER

Clam chowder is one of the earliest and most famous of the seafood stews from the North East. Potatoes found their way into clam chowder in the 18th century, but salt pork and onions were ingredients from the beginning.

PREPARATION TIME: 20 minutes

COOKING TIME: 5-6 minutes

SERVES: 6-8

INGREDIENTS

- ☐ 3 large New England potatoes, diced and parboiled
- ☐ 1 medium Spanish onion, chopped ☐ 12 quahogs
- ☐ 4 crushed black peppercorns ☐ 1 tsp fresh thyme
- ☐ 1 bay leaf ☐ 1 tsp fresh rosemary, chopped
- ☐ 1 tbsp fresh parsley, chopped ☐ 3 pints water
- ☐ 3oz butter or soaked salt pork

Cook the potatoes and if using salt pork, place it in a sauté pan over low heat to render the fat. Sauté the chopped onions in the pork fat or butter until soft. Meanwhile, steam the quahogs in water until they open. Save the juice and allow the clams to cool before chopping them. Add the herbs, spices, reserved clam juice, chopped clams and cooked potatoes to the onions and cook until the potatoes are soft and all the flavors are blended.

THE OLYMPIA TEA ROOM,
BAY STREET, WATCH HILL, RI

Facing page: Rhode Island Clam Chowder, photographed at Steven Mack's Chase Hill Farm, coastal Rhode Island. Above: near Brenton Point, rocky outcrops enclose the ruffled waters of Greens Pond.

NEW ENGLAND BOUILLABAISSE

French settlers brought this favorite recipe to the New World, and just as they would have at home, they used local, seasonal ingredients in it.

PREPARATION TIME: 35 minutes

COOKING TIME: 30 minutes

SERVES: 4

INGREDIENTS

STOCK

- ☐ 1lb fish bones, skin and heads   ☐ 7 cups water
- ☐ 1 small onion, thinly sliced
- ☐ 1 small carrot, thinly sliced   ☐ 1 bay leaf
- ☐ 6 black peppercorns   ☐ 1 blade mace
- ☐ 1 sprig thyme   ☐ 2 lemon slices

BOUILLABAISSE

- ⅓ cup butter or margarine ☐ 1 carrot, sliced
- 3 leeks, well washed and thinly sliced ☐ 1 clove garlic
- Pinch saffron ☐ ⅓ - ½ cup dry white wine
- 8oz canned tomatoes ☐ 1 lobster
- 1lb cod or halibut fillets ☐ 1lb mussels, well scrubbed
- 1lb small clams, well scrubbed ☐ 8 new potatoes, scrubbed but not peeled
- Chopped parsley ☐ 8oz large shrimp, peeled and de-veined

First prepare the fish stock. Place all the ingredients in a large stock pot and bring to the boil over high heat. Lower the heat and allow to simmer for 20 minutes. Strain and reserve the stock. Discard the fish bones and vegetables. Melt the butter in a medium-sized saucepan and add the carrots, leeks and garlic. Cook for about 5 minutes until slightly softened. Add the saffron and wine and allow to simmer for about 5 minutes. Add the fish stock along with all the remaining bouillabaisse ingredients except the shrimp. Bring the mixture to the boil and cook until the lobster turns red, the mussel and clam shells open and the potatoes are tender. Turn off the heat and add the shrimp. Cover the pan and let the shrimp cook in the residual heat. Divide the ingredients among 4 soup bowls. Remove the lobster and cut it in half. Divide the tail between the other 2 bowls and serve the bouillabaisse with garlic bread.

Facing page: New England Bouillabaisse. Above: a variety of pleasure craft moored in Newport Harbor.

BUTTER FISH

These are light, tasty fish caught in waters of New England. Leave on the head and tail and serve them on the griddle on which they are cooked. They are delicious for breakfast with scrambled eggs.

PREPARATION TIME: 20 minutes

COOKING TIME: 3 minutes

SERVES: 4

INGREDIENTS

☐ 4-8 butter fish, gutted ☐ 2-4 tbsps butter
☐ Lemon slices

Place 1-2 fish per person on a hot griddle with butter and cook over a low heat for about 3 minutes. The fish may not need to be turned. Garnish each fish with half a thin slice of lemon. Serve as a side dish at any meal.

STEVEN P. MACK, CHASE HILL FARM,
ASHAWAY, RI

Above: a spectacular sunset, caught just before the sun finally sinks below the horizon.
Facing page: Butter Fish, photographed at Steven Mack's Chase Hill Farm, coastal Rhode Island.

BAKED SEA TROUT IN PARCHMENT

Wrapping delicate food such as fish in paper parcels is an ingenious way of ensuring that all the flavors remain sealed in. For full effect, open the parcels at the table.

PREPARATION TIME: 25 minutes

COOKING TIME: 20 minutes

OVEN TEMPERATURE: 350°F

SERVES: 2

INGREDIENTS

☐ 1-1¼ lb sea trout fillet (any firm-fleshed fish will do)
☐ 4 cleaned mussels ☐ 4 Spanish onion slices
☐ 4 fresh tomato slices ☐ 4 green pepper rings
☐ 4 sprigs fresh thyme ☐ 4 sprigs fresh sage
☐ 2 crushed white peppercorns ☐ Melted butter
☐ White wine

Divide the fish into two equal portions and place skinned side down on parchment paper (foil will suffice, but it is not as attractive). Garnish the fish with onion slices, tomato slices and then pepper rings. Place the mussels on top and then the herbs and pepper. Drizzle a little melted butter and wine on the fish and then seal the paper parcels, twisting the ends well. Coat the outsides with additional melted butter and bake for about 20 minutes.

THE OLYMPIA TEA ROOM,
BAY STREET, WATCH HILL, RI

Facing page: Baked Sea Trout in Parchment, photographed at Steven Mack's Chase Hill Farm, coastal Rhode Island. Above: modeled on the 17th- and 18th-century architecture of Versailles, Marble House in Newport was built in 1892 for William K. Vanderbilt.

CHATEAUBRIAND (ROAST TENDERLOIN MADEIRA)

Hammersmith Farm has a long history. It was established in 1640 and throughout the years has been owned by just three families. Like the house and grounds where Jacqueline Bouvier had the reception after her wedding to John F. Kennedy, the recipe for Chateaubriand is truly elegant.

PREPARATION TIME: 40 minutes

COOKING TIME: 1 hour

SERVES: 6

INGREDIENTS

☐ 2-3lbs beef tenderloin in 1 piece ☐ Butter

MADEIRA SAUCE

☐ 1 cup beef consommé mixed with 2 tsps cornstarch ☐ ¼ cup dry Madeira
☐ ¼ cup butter

GARNISHES

☐ Baked stuffed potatoes with Parmesan cheese ☐ Small Belgian carrots
☐ Baby onions ☐ Asparagus ☐ Artichoke hearts

Above: looking toward Newport from the east.

─────── TOMATO TIMBALES WITH BROCCOLI───────

◻ 6 tomatoes   ◻ 6oz broccoli flowerets
◻ Parmesan cheese   ◻ 3 tbsps butter

Fold under the thin end of the meat and tie the tenderloin at intervals with thin string. Spread the meat with butter and roast on a rack in a roasting pan for 25 minutes in a moderate oven. Cook the carrots and onions in water for about 10 minutes. Add the asparagus and artichoke hearts after 5 minutes. Drain all the vegetables and sauté them in garlic butter to finish cooking. To prepare the timbales, blanch the broccoli flowerets in boiling salted water for 2 minutes. Cut off the rounded ends of the tomatoes and scoop out the pulp and seeds. Stuff with the blanched broccoli, sprinkle with Parmesan cheese and dot with butter. Bake in a moderate oven for 10 minutes. Prepare the baked stuffed potatoes in advance and finish cooking with the tomato and broccoli timbales. When the meat and garnishes are cooked, heat the consommé and the cornstarch in a small saucepan, stirring constantly until the mixture comes to the boil. Add the Madeira and cook until slightly thickened. Swirl in the butter and serve the sauce with the Chateaubriand.

CHEF PETER T. CROWLEY,
LA FORGE CASINO RESTAURANT,
NEWPORT, RI

Above: a line of rowing boats moored to a wooden pier at Newport Beach.

POACHED SALMON WITH DILL SAUCE

A whole poached fish is a stunning start to a meal. While looking very impressive, this salmon is easy to prepare and can be cooked ahead of time. The sauce finishes off the appetizer deliciously. A larger salmon makes a main dinner course on a warm summer evening.

PREPARATION TIME: 25 minutes

COOKING TIME: 15 minutes

SERVES: 6-8

INGREDIENTS

☐ 2-3lb whole salmon, cleaned

COURT BOUILLON

☐ 2 pints water ☐ ½ cup dry white wine
☐ ½ onion, diced ☐ 2 sticks celery, diced
☐ 1 carrot, diced ☐ 1 tbsp salt
☐ ½ tsp pepper ☐ 3 whole cloves
☐ 1 bay leaf ☐ ½ lemon, sliced
☐ 3 parsley sprigs

DILL SAUCE

☐ 4 cups sour cream ☐ 3 tbsps chopped fresh dill
☐ Juice of 1 small lemon ☐ ,Pinch salt
☐ Pinch white pepper ☐ 1 tsp horseradish

Combine the court bouillon ingredients in a large saucepan and bring to the boil. Lower the heat and simmer for 30-45 minutes, strain and allow to cool completely. Place the salmon in a large roasting pan or a fish kettle and pour over the cool court bouillon. Cover and simmer for 15 minutes or place in a preheated 375°F oven for 15 minutes. When the dorsal fin on the back pulls out easily, the fish is cooked. Do not over-cook as the fish will continue to cook slightly as it cools. Lift the fish out of the pan and peel off the skin while still warm. Carefully transfer to a large serving plate and allow to cool. Combine all the sauce ingredients and serve with the salmon. Decorate the plate with watercress if desired.

CHEF PETER T. CROWLEY,
LA FORGE CASINO RESTAURANT,
NEWPORT, RI

Facing page: Poached Salmon with Dill Sauce and Chateaubriand (Roast Tenderloin Madeira) form the basis of this formal dinner, photographed at Hammersmith Farm, Newport.

LEG OF LAMB ROASTED IN A REFLECTOR OVEN

Lamb is an ideal meat to cook by this method because its natural fat keeps the meat moist. The meat is at its best when it is slightly pink in the center. Rosemary complements the flavor of lamb well, but try thyme or mint for a taste variation.

PREPARATION TIME: 15 minutes

COOKING TIME: 1-1½ hours

SERVES: 6-8

INGREDIENTS

- 5-6lb leg of lamb
- 4 cloves garlic, halved or quartered depending upon size
- Fresh or dried rosemary, crushed

Push a sharp knife into the meat at 5 inch intervals and insert slivers of garlic into the cuts. Rub with rosemary. Pierce the leg with a skewer and place it in the oven. Cook in front of a slow fire at a distance of approximately 18 inches. Turn every 15 minutes while basting in its own juices. When the meat looks done, cut a small, deep slice to check the color.

STEVEN P. MACK, CHASE HILL FARM,
ASHAWAY, RI

Above: Leg of Lamb Roasted in a Reflector Oven, photographed at Steven Mack's Chase Hill Farm, coastal Rhode Island.

STEAK OVER OPEN FIRE

Chuck steak is a much ignored and inexpensive cut that is delicious when cooked in this manner. Remove the steak just before it is done as it will cook slightly after being taken off the heat. An overcooked steak is no steak at all! Joseph Mack of Chase Hill Farm is the true master of this dish.

PREPARATION TIME: 15 minutes

COOKING TIME: 10-20 minutes

SERVES: 4

INGREDIENTS

- ☐ 4 6-8oz chuck steaks, cut 1 inch thick
- ☐ 12-16 large mushroom caps
- ☐ 2 large onions, thickly sliced
- ☐ Sea salt, coarsely ground

Rub the sea salt on both sides of the meat and place on a skillet with the mushroom caps and onions. Place the skillet over a medium fire. The steaks should take only 10-20 minutes to cook, so make sure to cook them last. Turn the steaks only once while cooking and serve with the mushrooms and onions.

STEVEN P. MACK, CHASE HILL FARM,
ASHAWAY, RI

Above: Steak over Open Fire, photographed at Steven Mack's Chase Hill Farm, coastal Rhode Island.

GRAND MARNIER CAKE

PREPARATION TIME: 1 hour

COOKING TIME: 20-30 minutes

OVEN TEMPERATURE: 375°F

SERVES: 8

—————————— INGREDIENTS ——————————

———————————————— CAKE ————————————————

☐ 2¼ cups sugar   ☐ 12 eggs, separated
☐ 2¼ cups unsalted butter, melted
☐ ¾ cup all-purpose flour sifted with a pinch of salt
☐ Pinch cream of tartar   ☐ 6oz German sweet chocolate

———————————— CHOCOLATE CUPS ————————————

☐ 2oz semi-sweet baking chocolate   ☐ 1 tsp shortening
☐ Grand Marnier

———————————————— ICING ————————————————

☐ 2lbs unsalted butter   ☐ 1 cup shortening
☐ 1 cup milk   ☐ 2 cups powdered sugar, sifted
☐ 1 tsp vanilla   ☐ 2oz dark chocolate, melted

First grease and flour 3 8-inch round cake pans. Beat the sugar and egg yolks together until thick and lemon colored. Fold in the melted butter and sift in the flour, salt and cream of tartar. Fold together to mix thoroughly. Beat the egg whites until stiff but not dry. Fold into the cake mixture carefully. Do not over fold. Divide the mixture in thirds and fill 2 of the prepared cake pans with ⅔ of the mixture. Fold the melted chocolate into the remaining third and spoon into the remaining pan. Bake in a moderate oven until the mixture shrinks slightly from the sides of the pans and the tops spring back when touched lightly.

Meanwhile, prepare the chocolate cups. Chop the chocolate into small pieces and combine with the shortening in the top of a double boiler. Melt over gently simmering water, stirring occasionally. When the chocolate is melted, use a pastry brush to paint an even layer of chocolate in each of 8 paper candy cups. Allow to harden, chilling in the refrigerator if necessary.

While the cakes are cooling, prepare the icing. Beat the butter and shortening until light and fluffy. Sift in the powdered sugar and beat until creamy, adding the milk gradually. It may not be necessary to add all the milk. Melt the chocolate and allow it to cool slightly before adding it to ⅓ of the icing. Add vanilla to the remaining ⅔ of the icing.

To assemble the cake, cut the 3 layers in half, horizontally. Sandwich the layers together, alternating the chocolate and vanilla icings, saving enough vanilla icing for the top and sides of the cake. Peel the paper cups carefully away from the chocolate and fill each chocolate cup with Grand Marnier. Place the cups on top of the cake and decorate as shown.

CHEF PETER T. CROWLEY,
LA FORGE CASINO RESTAURANT,
NEWPORT, RI

Facing page: Photographed at Hammersmith Farm, Newport, this Grand Marnier Cake is based on a French gateau, but the liqueur-filled chocolate cups are an original addition.

STRAWBERRY CHEESECAKE

A cheesecake is a dessert that never fails to please. This recipe serves a large gathering, but can easily be cut in half. Strawberries are a favorite choice for topping and they complement the velvety texture so well. For shine, melt a little seedless raspberry jam and brush over the berries, if desired.

PREPARATION TIME: 30 minutes

COOKING TIME: 40 minutes

OVEN TEMPERATURE: 375°F

MAKES 2-10 inch cakes

INGREDIENTS

☐ 3lbs cream cheese or curd cheese ☐ 15 eggs
☐ ½ cup sour cream ☐ 1 tbsp vanilla extract

GRAHAM CRACKER CRUST

☐ 4 cups graham cracker crumbs ☐ 1⅓ cups sugar
☐ ½ lb butter, melted

TOPPING

☐ 1lb even-sized strawberries, hulled

Soften the cream cheese and gradually beat in the eggs. Stir in the sour cream and vanilla extract. Combine the crust ingredients in a food processor or bowl and mix thoroughly. Press into spring-form pans and pour in the filling. Cook in a moderate oven for 40 minutes. Allow to cool completely before removing from the pans. Decorate the top of each cake with strawberries and brush over jam, if desired.

CHEF PETER T. CROWLEY,
LA FORGE CASINO RESTAURANT,
NEWPORT, RI

Above: Newport Bridge stretches gracefully across Narragansett Bay.
Facing page: Strawberry Cheesecake, photographed at Hammersmith Farm, Newport.

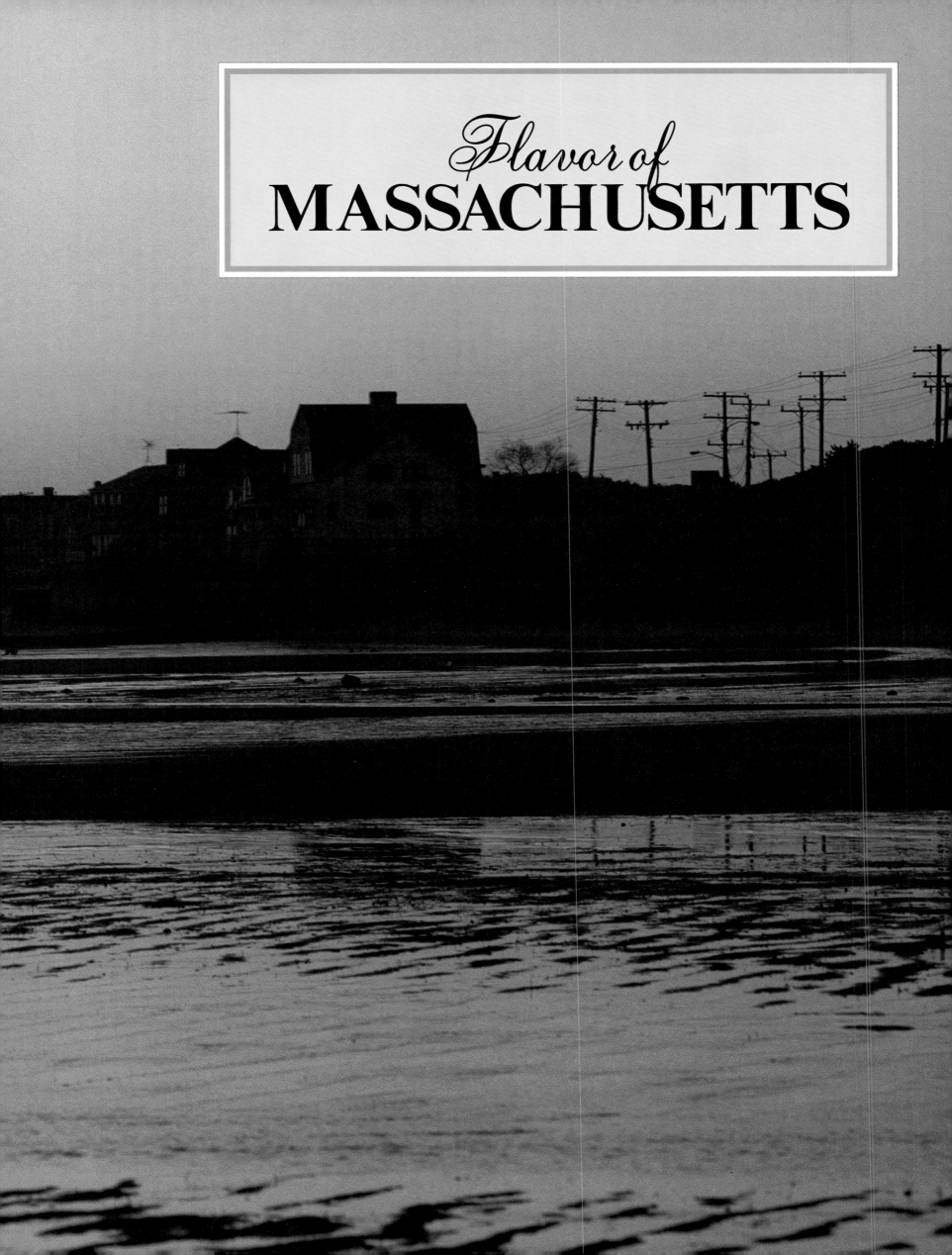

Flavor of
MASSACHUSETTS

VILLAGE INN HARVEST VEGETABLE SOUP

Soup was one of the mainstays of early American diets. This recipe is typical of the soups served in country villages when stock pots were kept going on the back of the stove all the time, and when villagers' own gardens provided the vegetables in the late summer and fall.

PREPARATION TIME: 25 minutes

COOKING TIME: 22 minutes

SERVES: 8

INGREDIENTS

- ☐ 3 cups strong veal stock   ☐ 3 cups strong chicken stock
- ☐ ½ tsp basil leaves   ☐ ½ tsp thyme leaves   ☐ 1 bay leaf
- ☐ ¼ tsp minced garlic   ☐ ¼ cup diced mushrooms
- ☐ ¼ cup clean chopped spinach   ☐ 2 tbsps tomato paste
- ☐ ¼ cup diced zucchini   ☐ ¼ cup diced summer squash
- ☐ ½ cup diced onions   ☐ ¼ cup diced carrots   ☐ ¼ cup diced celery
- ☐ ¼ cup broccoli flowerets   ☐ ¼ cup diced cabbage
- ☐ ¼ cup diced cauliflower flowerets   ☐ 3 tbsps butter

In a large stock pot, melt the butter and add the herbs, garlic, celery and carrots. Stir well and cook until the vegetables are beginning to soften but not browning. Add the onion, broccoli and cauliflower. Stir well and cook for 2 minutes. Add the zucchini, summer squash and mushrooms and cook for a further 2 minutes. Add the spinach and cabbage and mix well. Pour in the veal stock and chicken stock and add the tomato paste. Bring to the boil and stir occasionally. Reduce the heat and let the soup simmer for 20 minutes. Remove from the heat and add salt and pepper to taste. Let the soup cool to room temperature, cover and refrigerate overnight. The fat will rise to the surface and solidify, making it easy to remove. Spoon off the hardened fat and bring the soup back to the boil. Use your favorite garnish, such as grated cheese, croutons, or chopped parsley. Reheating and serving the soup the next day gives the flavors a chance to meld together.

CHEF JAMES E. LOWE,
THE VILLAGE INN,
LENOX, MA

Previous pages: the sun sets over Provincetown, Cape Cod.
Facing page: Village Inn Harvest Vegetable Soup and a side salad served with Monterey Chevre Dressing.
Overleaf: a selection of warming soups, with Cream of Tomato and Cheddar Soup in the foreground.

MONTEREY CHEVRE
DRESSING

*With the help of a food processor, this is a quickly-made salad dressing.
Prepare it well ahead of time for all the flavors to blend, and serve it with
your favorite salad greens. It is also delicious with sliced tomatoes or
spooned on top of a ripe avocado.*

PREPARATION TIME: 10 minutes

MAKES: 3 cups

INGREDIENTS

☐ 1 bunch scallions, washed   ☐ ¼ cup diced onion
☐ 6oz garlic and chive Chevre cheese (room temperature)
☐ ½ cup sour cream   ☐ ½ cup mayonnaise   ☐ 1 cup half and half

Cut the root ends off the scallions and chop the white portion and green tops into small
pieces. Purée in a food processor with the onion. Put the purée into a bowl with the
cheese, sour cream and mayonnaise. Mix together well with a wire whisk, making sure
the cheese is broken up and not lumpy. Beat in the half and half until the dressing is
smooth and creamy. Add salt and pepper to taste, if desired. Cover and refrigerate until
ready to serve. The dressing will thicken up considerably in the refrigerator, so thin with
additional half and half if necessary.

CHEF JAMES E. LOWE,
THE VILLAGE INN,
LENOX, MA

CREAM OF TOMATO AND CHEDDAR SOUP

Tomato soup used to be one of the more fashionable soups for a company dinner. Cheddar cheese used to be made in every state where there was a dairy industry and was a popular food across the country. With tomatoes and cheese being such a good combination, it was natural to bring them together in one delicious soup.

PREPARATION TIME: 25 minutes

COOKING TIME: 1 hour 10 minutes

SERVES: 12

INGREDIENTS

- □ 1 small onion, chopped   □ 4 stalks celery, leaves removed
- □ 3 carrots, peeled   □ 2lbs canned Italian plum tomatoes
- □ 3 tbsps whole mixed pickling spice tied in a small cheesecloth bag
- □ 4 tbsps extra virgin olive oil   □ 1 tsp Worcestershire sauce   □ ¼ tsp Tabasco
- □ 2 quarts veal stock
- □ ¾-1lb Vermont Cheddar cheese double aged (4 years) if possible, and shredded
- □ 5oz butter   □ 5oz flour □   □ 8oz butter
- □ 1 cup heavy cream   □ Salt and black pepper to taste

Chop the onions, celery and carrots finely. Sauté in the olive oil in a 1 gallon soup pot until slightly softened. Add the tomatoes, bag of spices, Worcestershire sauce and Tabasco and simmer for 1 hour, stirring often. Remove the spice bag and purée mixture in a food processor or food mill until smooth. Return to the rinsed out pan, add the veal stock and return the spice bag to the soup. Bring to the boil, reduce the heat and simmer until reduced by about a quarter. Put 5oz butter in a small saucepan and stir in the flour. Cook over low heat for 5 minutes, but do not brown. Gradually beat the roux into the soup and bring to the boil. Simmer for 10 minutes, add Cheddar cheese, remaining butter and cream. Adjust the seasonings and serve immediately. Garnish with croûtons, additional Cheddar cheese or chopped parsley, if desired.

CHEF STEPHEN MONGEON,
THE RED LION INN,
STOCKBRIDGE, MA

Above: the Soldiers' Monument was placed on the Common at Harvard University in 1870.
Facing page: Harvard Beets.

HARVARD BEETS

One of the best known dishes using this readily available root vegetable. The color makes this a perfect accompaniment to plain meat or poultry.

PREPARATION TIME: 20 minutes
COOKING TIME: 40-50 minutes, in total
SERVES: 6

INGREDIENTS

- 2lbs small beets
- Boiling water
- 3 tbsps cornstarch
- ½ cup sugar
- Pinch salt and pepper
- 1 cup white wine vinegar
- ¾ cup reserved beet cooking liquid
- 2 tbsps butter

Choose even-sized beets and cut off the tops, if necessary. Place beets in a large saucepan of water. Cover the pan and bring to the boil. Lower the heat and cook gently until tender, about 30-40 minutes. Add more boiling water as necessary during cooking. Drain the beets, reserving the liquid, and allow the beets to cool. When the beets are cool, peel them and slice into ¼ inch rounds, or cut into small dice. Combine the cornstarch, sugar, salt and pepper, vinegar and required amount of beet liquid in a large saucepan. Bring to the boil over moderate heat, stirring constantly until thickened. Return the beets to the saucepan and allow to heat through for about 5 minutes. Stir in the butter and serve immediately.

BOSTON
BAKED BEANS

In Colonial New England there were no fast food restaurants along the highways, so it was necessary for the traveler to carry his own provisions. In the winter, it was common for housewives to line a bean crock with cloth, pour in Boston baked beans and leave the crock outside to freeze. Frozen beans were easily lifted out and carried wrapped in the cloth. When the traveler was hungry, he broke off a chunk of the beans, thawed them out over his fire and ate them for his meal.

PREPARATION TIME: 20 minutes plus overnight soaking for the beans
COOKING TIME: 3 ½ hours
OVEN TEMPERATURE: 300°F
SERVES: 8

INGREDIENTS

□ 1lb package navy or pea beans
□ ¼ lb salt pork, cut into 2-inch pieces
□ 1 small whole onion, peeled   □ 1 tsp dry mustard   □ 6 cups water
□ ½ tsp baking soda   □ ⅓ cup molasses
□ 3 tbsps sugar   □ 1 tsp salt   □ ¼ tsp pepper

Soak the beans overnight in a large pot with 6 cups of water. Add the baking soda and bring to the boil. Allow to simmer 10 minutes, drain and reserve the liquid. Place the beans, salt pork and onion in a bean pot or casserole. Add the molasses, sugar, dry mustard, salt, pepper and a cup of the bean cooking liquid. Stir thoroughly and add enough liquid to cover the beans. Cover the bean pot or casserole with its lid. Bake 2 hours at 300°F. Add the remaining liquid and stir again. Bake additional 1 ½ hours or until the beans are tender. Uncover for the last ½ hour of cooking.

Facing Page: Boston Baked Beans.
Above: the State House in Boston was designed by Charles Bulfinch and completed in 1795.

STEAMED BROWN BREAD

This is the classic accompaniment to one of Boston's famous dishes – baked beans. It's traditional to bake it in a can!

PREPARATION TIME: 20 minutes

COOKING TIME: 3-4 hours

YIELD: 1 large loaf

— INGREDIENTS —

☐ 1½ cups fine cornmeal   ☐ 2 cups wholewheat flour   ☐ 1 cup all-purpose flour
☐ Pinch salt   ☐ ⅓ cup molasses mixed with 1 tsp bicarbonate of soda
☐ 1½ cups cold water   ☐ Butter or oil   ☐ Boiling water

Sift the dry ingredients into a large bowl and return the bran to the bowl. Mix the molasses, bicarbonate of soda and water together. Make a well in the center of the flour and pour in the mixture. Mix just until well blended. Use a large can from canned tomatoes, coffee or canned fruit. Alternatively, use about 6 smaller cans. Wash them well and remove the labels. Grease generously with oil or butter. Spoon the bread mixture to come about two thirds of the way up the sides of the cans. Cover the tops of the cans tightly with buttered or oiled foil. Place them on a rack in a deep saucepan. Pour enough boiling water around the cans to come about halfway up the sides. Allow water to bubble gently to steam the bread for 3-4 hours in the covered pan. Add more boiling water as necessary during cooking. The bread is ready when a skewer inserted into the center of the bread comes out clean.

*Facing page: these weathered logs are lying on the beach at Martha's Vineyard.
Above: Steamed Brown Bread.*

SCALLOP AND AVOCADO SEVICHE

The scallops in this recipe "cook" in the refrigerator! This dish is simple to prepare and makes a delicious first course. It will keep for 1 week in the refrigerator if stirred daily.

PREPARATION TIME: 20 minutes plus 36-48 hours in the refrigerator

SERVES: 6

INGREDIENTS

☐ 2lbs scallops, sliced   ☐ Juice of 5 limes   ☐ 1 cup salad oil
☐ 2 tomatoes, peeled, seeded and diced   ☐ 2 green peppers, diced
☐ 1 avocado, diced   ☐ ½ Spanish onion, minced   ☐ 2 cloves garlic, crushed
☐ ¾ tsp cayenne pepper   ☐ 1 tbsp white vinegar   ☐ 1 tsp salt

Combine all the ingredients and refrigerate. Cover the bowl and allow to marinate 36-48 hours, or until the scallops are opaque all the way through. Stir the seviche daily. Serve on lettuce leaves on individual plates.

NEAL SOLOMON, EXECUTIVE CHEF,
HAMPSHIRE HOUSE,
BEACON STREET, BOSTON, MA

Above: Martha's Vineyard has a variety of scenery, including these spectacular red clay cliffs.

CLAMS CASINO

There have been many different versions of this delicious clam dish, but green pepper and bacon are two of the original ingredients. Oysters can be cooked in the same way.

PREPARATION TIME: 25 minutes
COOKING TIME: 5-7 minutes
OVEN TEMPERATURE: 350°F
MAKES: 6 stuffed clams

INGREDIENTS

- ☐ ½ cup butter or margarine
- ☐ ½ oz diced green pepper
- ☐ ½ oz diced red pepper or pimento
- ☐ ½ oz diced onion
- ☐ 2-3 drops Tabasco sauce
- ☐ ¼ tsp Worcestershire sauce
- ☐ 3 slices bacon

Place the butter, peppers, pimento and onion in a mixing bowl and blend thoroughly by hand until the butter is softened and all the ingredients are incorporated. Mix in the Tabasco and Worcestershire sauce. Slice the bacon in half and set it aside. Spoon the butter mixture on top of the clams and place a half slice of bacon on top. Bake in a moderate oven for approximately 5-7 minutes, or until heated through and the bacon is crisp.

UNION OYSTER HOUSE,
BOSTON, MA

Above: "Peacefield" in Quincy was the home of President John Adams for forty years. Overleaf, from left: Clams Casino, Oysters Rockefeller and Baked Stuffed Cherrystones, photographed at the Union Oyster House, Boston.

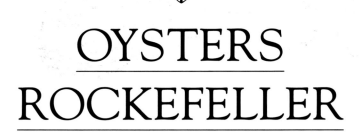

OYSTERS
ROCKEFELLER

This recipe has become a classic. It makes a luxurious first course, especially with the price of oysters! Perhaps that is why it carries the name of one of the wealthiest families in the United States.

PREPARATION TIME: 25 minutes
COOKING TIME: 12-15 minutes
OVEN TEMPERATURE: 350°F
MAKES: 6 oysters

––––––––––––––––– I N G R E D I E N T S –––––––––––––––––

☐ 1lb fresh spinach or ½ lb frozen chopped spinach
☐ 6 oysters on the half shell   ☐ ½ cup grated cheese

––––––––––––––– F I S H   V E L O U T É   S A U C E –––––––––––––––

☐ 1½ tbsps butter   ☐ 1½ tbsps flour   ☐ Pinch salt and white pepper
☐ ½ cup fish stock or clam juice   ☐ 2 tsps Poupon mustard

If using fresh spinach, wash well and remove any thick stalks. Place in a saucepan with a tight-fitting lid with a pinch of salt. Cook just until the leaves begin to wilt, remove from the heat, drain and press in a colander to remove all the water. Chop by hand or in a food processor and return to the pan over heat. Cook for 1 minute to evaporate any remaining liquid. If using frozen spinach, do not re-cook. Drain it very well and place in the pan for 1 minute over heat to dry. To prepare the sauce, melt the butter in a small saucepan and stir in the flour. Cook for 1-2 minutes, stirring constantly until a pale straw color. Gradually whisk in the stock, add salt and pepper and bring back to the boil. Allow to simmer 1-2 minutes or until thickened. Combine with the mustard and stir into the spinach. Spoon the spinach mixture on top of each oyster and sprinkle on the greated cheese. Bake in a moderate oven for 10-12 minutes and heat through to melt the cheese. Alternatively, top the spinach with Hollandaise sauce.

UNION OYSTER HOUSE,
BOSTON, MA

Facing page: Gay Head Cliffs, Martha's Vineyard.

BAKED STUFFED
CHERRYSTONES

*Cherrystones are hard-shelled clams found in abundance off the coast
of Massachusetts and all along the Eastern seaboard. Filled with a
flavorful stuffing, they make a delicious first course.*

PREPARATION TIME: 25 minutes

COOKING TIME: 10-12 minutes

OVEN TEMPERATURE: 350°F

MAKES: 6 stuffed clams

INGREDIENTS

☐ 6 tbsps butter or margarine   ☐ 2 tbsps diced onion
☐ 2 tbsps diced green pepper   ☐ 6 mushrooms, thinly sliced
☐ Pinch dry mustard   ☐ Pinch garlic powder   ☐ ¼ tsp oregano
☐ 2 tbsps clam juice   ☐ 4 tbsps water
☐ Bread crumbs   ☐ 6 cherrystone clams on the half shell

Put the butter in a small pan and sauté the onions, peppers and mushrooms until done.
Add mustard, garlic, oregano and a pinch of salt and pepper. Stir in the water and the clam
juice and bring to the boil. Remove from the heat and add enough bread crumbs to bring
the mixture together. Allow it to cool and spoon the mixture on the clams. Bake in their
shells for 10-12 minutes in a moderate oven.

UNION OYSTER HOUSE,
BOSTON, MA

SHRIMP SCAMPI CANDLELIGHT

Scampi are not really shrimp but Dublin Bay Prawns or langoustines, which were once plentiful in the Bay of Naples. These shellfish are not native to American waters although shrimp, prepared in one of the same ways as scampi, makes a delicious substitute.

PREPARATION TIME: 15 minutes

COOKING TIME: 8-10 minutes

OVEN TEMPERATURE: 400°F

SERVES: 4

INGREDIENTS

☐ 16 large shrimp, cut down the middle, cleaned and left in their shells

SAUCE

☐ 8oz butter, melted   ☐ 2 cloves garlic, crushed
☐ 2 tbsps tarragon, chopped   ☐ 2 tsps Dijon mustard   ☐ Dash A-1 sauce
☐ Dash Worcestershire sauce   ☐ Dash Tabasco   ☐ Dash red wine vinegar
☐ 1 large tbsp sour cream   ☐ Dash lemon juice

Place the shrimp in an ovenproof dish and combine all the sauce ingredients. Beat well and pour over the shrimp. Cook for 8-10 minutes, or until the shrimp shells turn pink.

MARSHA HELLER, CHEF,
CANDLELIGHT INN, MA

Facing Page: Shrimp Scampi Candlelight. Above: fishing boats in Provincetown, which is no longer a whaling center, but still prospers as a commercial fishing port.

BOSTON SCROD

Scrod, or baby codfish, provides the perfect base for a crunchy, slightly spicy topping. Boston is justly famous for it.

PREPARATION TIME: 15 minutes

COOKING TIME: 12 minutes

SERVES: 4

INGREDIENTS

□ 4 even-sized cod fillets   □ Salt and pepper
□ ⅓ cup butter, melted   □ ¾ cup dry breadcrumbs
□ 1 tsp dry mustard   □ 1 tsp onion salt
□ Dash Worcestershire sauce and tabasco   □ 2 tbsps lemon juice
□ 1 tbsp finely chopped parsley

Season the fish fillets with salt and pepper and place them on a broiler tray. Brush with butter and broil for about 5 minutes. Combine remaining butter with breadcrumbs, mustard, onion salt, Worcestershire sauce, tabasco, lemon juice and parsley. Spoon the mixture carefully on top of each fish fillet, covering it completely. Press down lightly to pack the crumbs into place. Broil for a further 5-7 minutes, or until the top is lightly browned and the fish flakes.

Above: Boston Scrod. Facing page: the outgoing tide has left this boat high and dry on Little Neck beach.

LOBSTER THERMIDOR

Lobsters were common fare for the Pilgrims even though they have now become a luxury. American or Northern lobsters live only on the Eastern coast of North America and thrive in the cold water. Be sure to choose a lobster which is heavy in weight in proportion to its size. This indicates that it will be a meaty and well flavored one.

PREPARATION TIME: 40 minutes
COOKING TIME: 25 minutes
SERVES: 1

INGREDIENTS

- ☐ 1¼ lb whole cooked lobster
- ☐ ¾ cup heavy cream
- ☐ 1 egg yolk
- ☐ Salt and pepper
- ☐ Pinch cayenne pepper
- ☐ 1 tbsp sherry
- ☐ ½ a small green pepper, sliced
- ☐ ½ a small red pimento, sliced
- ☐ 1oz sliced mushrooms
- ☐ 1 tbsp Dijon mustard

HOLLANDAISE SAUCE

- ☐ 1 egg yolk
- ☐ 2oz butter, melted
- ☐ Dash lemon juice
- ☐ Pinch salt and pepper
- ☐ 2 tbsps grated cheese

GARNISH

- ☐ Black olives
- ☐ Mashed potato
- ☐ Lemon wedges

Cut the lobster in half lengthwise and loosen the tail meat but do not remove. Crack the large claws and remove all the meat. Remove the legs and extract as much meat as possible from them. Clean out the body cavity of the lobster. (The green tomally or liver may be eaten, as can the roe or coral.) Pour the heavy cream into a small saucepan and bring to the boil. Add salt, pepper and sherry and reduce the cream by a ¼ . Beat the egg yolks and beat in a spoonful of the hot cream. Pour the egg yolks into the cream in the saucepan and cook over gentle heat, stirring continuously until it just coats the back of a spoon. Sauté the peppers, pimentos and mushrooms in about 1 tbsp of butter until cooked. Add the lobster claw meat and any meat from the legs to the vegetables and stir in the mustard. Pour on the sauce and keep warm.

Meanwhile, prepare the Hollandaise sauce. Place the egg yolk and the lemon juice and a pinch of salt and pepper in a blender. Heat the butter until bubbling and, with the machine running, pour the butter in through the funnel gradually. Set the sauce aside. To assemble, pipe a border of the mashed potatoes on a large ovenproof plate and brown under a preheated broiler. Place the lobster, cut side up, in the center of the potato border. Spoon the thermidor sauce into the body cavity and coat some over the tail. Spoon the Hollandaise sauce on top of the thermidor sauce and sprinkle with grated cheese. Place in the oven or under the broiler until golden brown on top. Decorate the potato border with lemons and olives and serve immediately.

UNION OYSTER HOUSE,
BOSTON, MA

Previous pages: Lobster Thermidor, photographed at the Union Oyster House, Boston. Facing page: Cape Cod Mussels.

CAPE COD MUSSELS

When seafood is as good as that from Cape Cod, even the simplest preparations stand out.

PREPARATION TIME: 30 minutes

COOKING TIME: 5-8 minutes

SERVES: 4

INGREDIENTS

- 4½ lbs mussels in their shells
- Flour or cornmeal
- 1 cup dry white wine
- 1 large onion, finely chopped
- 2-4 cloves garlic, finely chopped
- Salt and coarsely ground black pepper
- 2 bay leaves
- 1 cup butter, melted
- Juice of 1 lemon

Scrub the mussels well and remove any barnacles and beards (seaweed strands). Use a stiff brush to scrub the shells, and discard any mussels with broken shells or those that do not close when tapped. Place the mussels in a basin full of cold water with a handful of flour or cornmeal and leave to soak for 30 minutes. Drain the mussels and place them in a large, deep saucepan with the remaining ingredients, except the butter and lemon juice. Cover the pan and bring to the boil. Stir the mussels occasionally while they are cooking to help them cook evenly. Cook about 5-8 minutes, or until the shells open. Discard any mussels that do not open. Spoon the mussels into individual serving bowls and strain the cooking liquid. Pour the liquid into 4 small bowls and serve with the mussels and a bowl of melted butter mixed with lemon juice for each person. Dip the mussels into the broth and the melted butter to eat. Use a mussel shell to scoop out each mussel, or eat with small forks or spoons.

CAPE SCALLOP

BROCHETTE

Scallops were said to be the emblem of the pilgrims who visited the shrine of St. James in Compostella. They were given scallops to eat as a penance, surely not an unpleasant one! Sea scallops are usually quite large, so cut them in half, if necessary, so that they cook in the same time as the vegetables.

PREPARATION TIME: 20 minutes

COOKING TIME: 10-15 minutes

SERVES: 4

INGREDIENTS

□ 1¼ lbs fresh sea scallops   □ 16 cherry tomatoes
□ 8 large mushrooms   □ 1 large green pepper, cut in large pieces
□ 1 onion, cut in quarters   □ 12 bacon slices

MARINADE

□ ¾ cup vegetable oil   □ ¼ cup wine vinegar   □ 1 clove garlic, crushed
□ Pinch oregano   □ Pinch basil   □ Pinch parsley

Wrap the scallops in the bacon. Separate the layers of onions and alternate on skewers with the scallops in bacon and the other vegetables. Mix the marinade ingredients together and brush over the brochettes. Broil on hot coals or under a preheated broiler, basting frequently with the marinade for about 10-15 minutes, or until the scallops are cooked and the bacon is crisp.

MARSHA HELLER, CHEF,
CANDLELIGHT INN, MA

Above: Cape Scallop Brochette. Facing page: the 251-foot-high Pilgrim Monument at Provincetown commemorates the Pilgrims' landing here before they moved on to Plymouth.

SHAKER STYLE CHICKEN BREASTS WITH A CIDER SAUCE

The Shakers were a religious community that flourished in late 18th and early 19th century in the United States. They were dedicated to productive labour and to a life of perfection. The style of cooking was based on good, honest ingredients.

PREPARATION TIME: 25 minutes

COOKING TIME: 30 minutes

OVEN TEMPERATURE: 350°F

SERVES: 4

INGREDIENTS

☐ 2 whole chicken breasts with wings attached ☐ Flour for dusting
☐ ½ cup apple cider ☐ ½ cup apple cider vinegar
☐ 2 tbsps honey ☐ ¾ cup heavy cream ☐ 1 apple, peeled, cored and diced
☐ 3 tbsps minced parsley ☐ 2 tbsps butter

Skin and bone the chicken breasts, leaving the wings attached. Cut off the wings at the second joint and cut the breasts in half lengthwise. Salt and pepper the chicken and dust lightly with flour. Heat the butter in an ovenproof pan and brown the breasts skin side down first. Turn over and place the chicken breasts in the oven. Bake for about 20 minutes, or until cooked through but not dry. Remove the chicken to a hot platter and cover with foil to keep warm. Pour off almost all the fat from the pan and sauté the diced apple until golden brown. Remove the apples to drain on paper towels. Pour off any remaining liquid from the pan and add the honey and vinegar. Reduce over a medium heat until the liquid is almost a glaze, being careful not to let it boil over. Take the pan off the heat and add the apple cider slowly, stirring in gradually. Return the pan to medium heat and continue cooking to reduce by about ¾. Be careful not to let the liquid burn. Pour in the heavy cream and cook over high heat to reduce slightly. To serve, cut wings off the breasts and place them at the top center of each serving plate. Cap each wing with a paper frill. Slice the rest of the chicken breasts into thin slices, using the wing tips as the center point, and fan the chicken slices out on the plates. Divide the sauce evenly among the plates. Sprinkle the diced apple over the chicken and add some chopped parsley. Serve with quartered sautéed mushrooms or your favorite vegetable.

CHEF JAMES E. LOWE,
THE VILLAGE INN,
LENOX, MA

Facing page: Shaker Style Chicken Breasts with a Cider Sauce.

ROAST DUCKLING WITH CRANBERRIES, ORANGES AND MINT

This is an elegant recipe for duckling from a restaurant on Beacon Hill, Boston's most fashionable area. Beacon Hill is also one of the oldest residential areas in Boston and maintains its charm to this day.

PREPARATION TIME: 30 minutes

COOKING TIME: 1½-1¾ hours

OVEN TEMPERATURE: 425°F

SERVES: 3-4

INGREDIENTS

- 1 whole fresh duckling, 4-5lbs in weight
- ¾ cup dry sherry
- ¼ cup soy sauce
- 1lb cranberries
- 3 tbsps butter
- Sugar to taste

SAUCE

- 4 cups good veal stock
- 1 cup dry sherry
- 1 tbsp finely chopped shallots
- 3 tbsps butter
- 3 tbsps flour
- 2 bunches fresh mint, washed and chopped

GARNISH

- Sliced oranges
- Fresh mint

Remove the giblets from the duck and cut off the wing tips. Prick the skin all over with a sharp knife. Combine the sherry and soy sauce and pour over the duck to marinate, uncovered, for 24 hours in the refrigerator. Place one oven rack in the center of a preheated oven. Adjust the second rack in the lower third of the oven. Place on it a large pan filled with ½ inch of water. Pat the duck dry and place directly on the upper oven rack so that drippings will fall into the pan of water below. Cook until the legs move freely in their joints and the drippings in the cavity are clear.

To prepare the sauce, melt the butter in a saucepan and cook the shallots until translucent. Add the flour and cook 3-4 minutes, stirring constantly. Reduce the veal stock and the sherry to about ⅓ and stir into the flour and butter roux. Allow to boil until slightly thickened and remove from the heat. Add the mint and allow to stand for 10 minutes. Strain and season with salt and pepper and keep it warm. To finish, heat the remaining 3 tbsps butter in a deep saucepan and add the cranberries. Reduce the heat and allow the cranberries to cook briefly until just softened but not breaking up. Stir in sugar to taste and, when the duck is cooked, fill the cavity with the cooked cranberries. Line a warm serving platter with sliced oranges and place the duck on top. Pour the sauce over the duck and garnish with bunches of fresh mint.

NEAL SOLOMON, EXECUTIVE CHEF, HAMPSHIRE HOUSE,
BEACON STREET, BOSTON, MA

Facing page: Scallop and Avocado Seviche is to be followed here by Roast Duckling with Cranberries, Oranges and Mint. The delicious fruit tarts for dessert were supplied by David Berger, Fine European Cakes, Medford.

❧

CHICKEN POT PIE

*There are many versions of this pie to be found all over the country.
This recipe uses chicken especially prepared for the pie,
but left-over chicken can be used as well. The topping of buttermilk biscuits
makes this a real country-style pie.*

PREPARATION TIME: 35 minutes

COOKING TIME: 40-50 minutes

SERVES: 6

—————— I N G R E D I E N T S ——————
—————— P I E   F I L L I N G ——————

☐ 4 chicken breasts ☐ 1½ quarts water ☐ ½ tsp rosemary
☐ 1 clove garlic, crushed ☐ 2 bay leaves ☐ ½ tsp thyme
☐ ¼ tsp tarragon ☐ 4 whole black peppercorns ☐ 24 pearl onions
☐ 1 cup peas ☐ 2 carrots, peeled and diced ☐ 2 fl oz white wine

Above: Chicken Pot Pie.

BISCUIT TOPPING

- ☐ 3½ cups all-purpose flour   ☐ 1 tbsp plus 1 tsp baking powder
- ☐ Good pinch salt   ☐ 7 tbsps butter   ☐ 1¼ cups buttermilk
- ☐ Egg wash (1 whole egg and 1 tbsp water beaten until frothy)

To prepare the filling, combine the chicken, water, wine, garlic, herbs and peppercorns in a large saucepan and bring to the boil. Skim the top and reduce the heat. Allow to simmer 20-30 minutes, or until the chicken is tender. Remove the chicken from the pot and allow it to cool. Skin and remove the meat from the bone. Return the bones to the stock. Simmer the stock until reduced by half. Strain the stock and bring back to the boil. Blend 4 tbsps of butter and 4 tbsps of flour and cook over low heat for 5 minutes without browning. Beat the stock gradually into this mixture. Simmer for 10 minutes. Cook the carrots and onions in separate pots of boiling water until tender. Dice the chicken and combine with all the remaining ingredients in individual crocks.

Meanwhile, prepare the biscuits. Preheat the oven to 400°F and combine all the dry ingredients in a bowl. Cut in the butter until the mixture has the consistency of small peas. Add the buttermilk, stirring in gradually. On a floured board, roll out the dough about ½ to ¾ inch thick. Cut with a floured biscuit cutter and brush each round with the egg wash. Bake for 25-30 minutes or until golden brown. When the biscuits are removed from the oven, brush with melted butter. Place one biscuit on top of each crock of chicken filling. Cook through in the oven until piping hot and serve immediately.

CHEF STEPHEN MONGEON,
THE RED LION INN,
STOCKBRIDGE, MA

Above: the lighthouse at Edgartown, Martha's Vineyard.

ROAST PRIME RIBS OF BEEF RED LION

*The Red Lion in the recipe title refers to the Red Lion Inn in Stockbridge,
Massachusetts, located in the picturesque Berkshire Hills.
This recipe reflects the British heritage of the region.*

PREPARATION TIME: 2 hours
COOKING TIME: 3-3 hours 15 minutes
OVEN TEMPERATURE: as indicated in the methods
SERVES: 12

INGREDIENTS

BEEF

- ☐ 1 7-rib, 22-24lbs Black Angus Prime Rib with fat cap
- ☐ 4 fl oz Worcestershire sauce

RED LION SEASONING

- ☐ 3 ½ tbsps salt   ☐ ½ tbsp ground white pepper
- ☐ ½ tbsp ground black pepper   ☐ 1 tbsp coarse garlic powder
- ☐ 1 tbsp leaf thyme

POPOVERS
(individually prepared Yorkshire puddings)

- ☐ 6 large eggs   ☐ 4 cups all-purpose flour   ☐ ½ tsp salt
- ☐ ¼ tsp garlic powder   ☐ ⅛ tsp ground white pepper
- ☐ 12 fl oz beef drippings from the roasting pan

AU JUS

- ☐ 2 tbsps beef drippings (from roasting the meat)
- ☐ 2 small onions, chopped   ☐ 1 large carrot, chopped
- ☐ 3 stalks celery with leaves, chopped   ☐ 1 pint tawny or ruby port
- ☐ 1 medium Spanish onion, sliced in half horizontally
- ☐ 2 quarts well flavored beef broth   ☐ 3 whole cloves   ☐ 1 clove garlic, crushed
- ☐ 2 bay leaves   ☐ 1 tsp thyme

Preheat the oven to 350°F for the beef. Leave the beef at room temperature for 1 hour before roasting. Prick the fat with a sharp fork and rub the top and sides thoroughly with Worcestershire sauce. Rub all of the Red Lion seasoning into the fat cap. Place the ribs in a shallow roasting pan with the fat cap facing up. Let the beef stand for an additional 2 hours at room temperature to contribute to the flavor and tenderness. Roast the beef for approximately 3 to 3 ¼ hours, or to an internal temperature of 120°F. Remove the roast from the pan and keep in a warm, draught-free area for 30 to 40 minutes before carving. Take out all but 2 tbsp of the drippings from the pan and reserve the remaining for popovers.

Facing page: Roast Prime Ribs of Beef Red Lion.

To prepare the popovers, increase the oven temperature to 450°F. Combine all the ingredients and blend slightly with a whisk. The mixture will still be slightly lumpy. Add 2 tbsps of the beef drippings to each of 12 muffin pan cups. Place the pans in the oven and heat to a smoking point. Fill the cups not more than ⅓ full with batter. Place in the oven for 10 minutes. Do not open the oven door to check for at least 10 minutes. Reduce the oven temperature to 350°F and cook an additional 15 minutes, or until the popovers are golden brown. Turn off the oven and leave the door open. Remove the popovers from the pan and place them on a warm serving platter in the oven. Add the reserved 2 tbsps of beef drippings to the roasting pan along with the chopped onions, carrot and celery. Sauté gently in the pan for 5 minutes. Add the tawny or ruby port and bring to the boil. Reduce by about ⅓. Take half of the Spanish onion and cook over an open flame and add to the pan. Add the beef broth and all the remaining ingredients. Bring to the boil, reduce slightly and strain.

To serve, place the beef on a large serving platter and garnish with oven-roasted vegetables. Serve the popovers on the side. Complement the dish by preparing a sauce-boat of horseradish cream sauce and serve with the Au Jus separately. Slice the meat, alternating between slices on the bone and slices off the bone.

CHEF STEPHEN MONGEON,
THE RED LION INN,
STOCKBRIDGE, MA

CHOCOLATE CAKE

*Long ago a clever cook discovered that chocolate combined better
if melted with other ingredients, so this method of making a
chocolate cake is not a new one. It is often called Devil's Food Cake
for the obvious reason that it is sinfully good.*

PREPARATION TIME: 25 minutes
COOKING TIME: 30-35 minutes
OVEN TEMPERATURE: 350°F
MAKES: 1 3 layer cake

INGREDIENTS

□ 1½ cups milk   □ 4 squares unsweetened chocolate
□ 1½ cups sugar   □ ½ cup butter   □ 1 tsp vanilla extract   □ 2 eggs
□ 2 cups sifted flour   □ ¾ tsp salt   □ 1 tsp baking soda

ICING

□ 5 cups sifted confectioners' sugar   □ Water

DECORATION

□ Chocolate shavings

Line the bottom of 13″ x 8″ x 2″ baking pan with waxed paper, then grease and flour the paper. Place 1 cup of milk, the chocolate and half a cup of sugar in the top of a double boiler. Place over boiling water and cook, stirring constantly, until the chocolate is melted. Remove from the boiling water and allow to cool. Cream the butter and remaining sugar in a large mixing bowl with an electric mixer. Add the vanilla extract and eggs and beat well. Beat in the cooled chocolate mixture. Sift the flour with the salt and add to the chocolate mixture, alternating with the remaining milk. Beat for 2 minutes on medium speed. Dissolve the soda in 3 tbsps of boiling water. Add to the cake batter and beat for 1 minute longer. Pour into the prepared pan and bake for 30-35 minutes, or until a skewer inserted into the center of the cake comes out clean. Cool in the pan for 10 minutes and then remove to a wire rack to cool completely. Trim the edge of the cake and split into 3 layers, horizontally.

To prepare the icing, sift the sugar into a large mixing bowl and stir in enough water to bring to a spreading consistency. Sandwich the layers together with the frosting and frost the top of the cake as well. Sprinkle with the shaved chocolate before the icing is completely set on top.

MARSHA HELLER, CHEF,
CANDLELIGHT INN, MA

Facing page: this Chocolate Cake is totally irresistible.

STEAMED CRANBERRY PUDDING

Colonial women brought their favorite recipes with them and learned to adapt them to the local produce, hence an English steamed pudding with American cranberries.

PREPARATION TIME: 30-40 minutes

COOKING TIME: 1½ hours

SERVES: 6

INGREDIENTS

☐ 1½ cups all-purpose flour ☐ 2 tsps baking powder
☐ Pinch salt ☐ 1 cup chopped cranberries
☐ 1 small piece candied ginger, finely chopped ☐ 2 eggs, well beaten
☐ ½ cup honey ☐ 6 tbsps milk
☐ Grated juice and rind of 1 orange ☐ Grated juice and rind of ½ lemon
☐ ½ cup sugar ☐ 1 tbsp cornstarch ☐ ¾ cup water
☐ 1 tbsp butter or margarine

Sift the dry ingredients together in a large bowl. Toss in the cranberries and ginger. Mix the eggs, honey and milk together and gradually stir into the dry ingredients and the cranberries. Do not over stir. The mixture should not be uniformly pink. The mixture should be of thick dropping consistency. Add more milk if necessary. Spoon the mixture into a well-buttered pudding basin or bowl, cover with buttered foil and tie the top securely. Place the bowl on a rack in a pan of boiling water to come halfway up the sides. Cover the pan and steam the pudding for about 1½ hours, or until a skewer inserted into the center comes out clean. Leave to cool in the basin or bowl for about 10 minutes, loosen the edge with a knife and turn out onto a plate. Meanwhile, place the sugar and cornstarch into a saucepan with the orange juice and rind and lemon juice and rind. Add the water, stirring to blend well. Bring to the boil and allow to simmer until clear. Beat in the butter at the end and serve with the pudding.

Facing page: Steamed Cranberry Pudding. Above: the setting sun reflects off the water and buildings of Boston, as rowers and sailors enjoy the last of the day on the Charles River.

CRANBERRY NUT BREAD

Sassamanesh was the peculiar sounding Indian name for the delicious and versatile cranberry.

PREPARATION TIME: 20 minutes

COOKING TIME: 1 hour

OVEN TEMPERATURE: 325°F

MAKES: 1 loaf

INGREDIENTS

☐ 2 cups flour ☐ 2 tsp baking powder ☐ 1 cup sugar
☐ ½ tsp salt ☐ 1 tsp baking soda ☐ ½ cup orange juice
☐ 2 tbsps shortening, melted and cooled ☐ 4 tbsps water
☐ 1 whole egg ☐ 1½ cups chopped cranberries
☐ ½ cup chopped walnuts

Sift the dry ingredients into a large bowl. Combine the orange juice, shortening, water and egg and stir gradually into the dry ingredients. Fold the chopped cranberries and walnuts into the batter and pour into a greased and floured 9″ x 5″ x 2¾″ bread pan. Bake for 1 hour, or until a skewer inserted into the center comes out clean.

Previous pages: Cranberry Walnut Pie and Cranberry Nut Bread, recipes supplied by The Sheraton Plymouth Inn & Conference Center and prepared by Chef Robert T. Allan. Above: a cranberry bog. Facing page: Menemsha Harbor, Martha's Vineyard.

CRANBERRY WALNUT PIE

Colonial cooks often made cranberry tarts, so this would not be out of place at a Thanksgiving celebration.

PREPARATION TIME: 25 minutes
COOKING TIME: 1 hour
OVEN TEMPERATURE: 400°F reduced to 350°F
MAKES: 1 10-inch pie

INGREDIENTS

Favorite recipe for 10-inch 1-crust pasty shell

FILLING

☐ 6 Granny Smith apples, peeled, cored and sliced
☐ 3 cups cranberries, roughly chopped   ☐ ½ cup sugar   ☐ 1 tsp cinnamon
☐ ¼ tsp nutmeg   ☐ ¼ cup flour   ☐ 1 cup walnuts, chopped   ☐ Pinch salt

Combine all the filling ingredients and mix thoroughly. Spoon into the unbaked pie shell. Bake for 15 minutes at 400°F. Reduce the heat to 350°F and bake an additional 45 minutes. Serve warm.

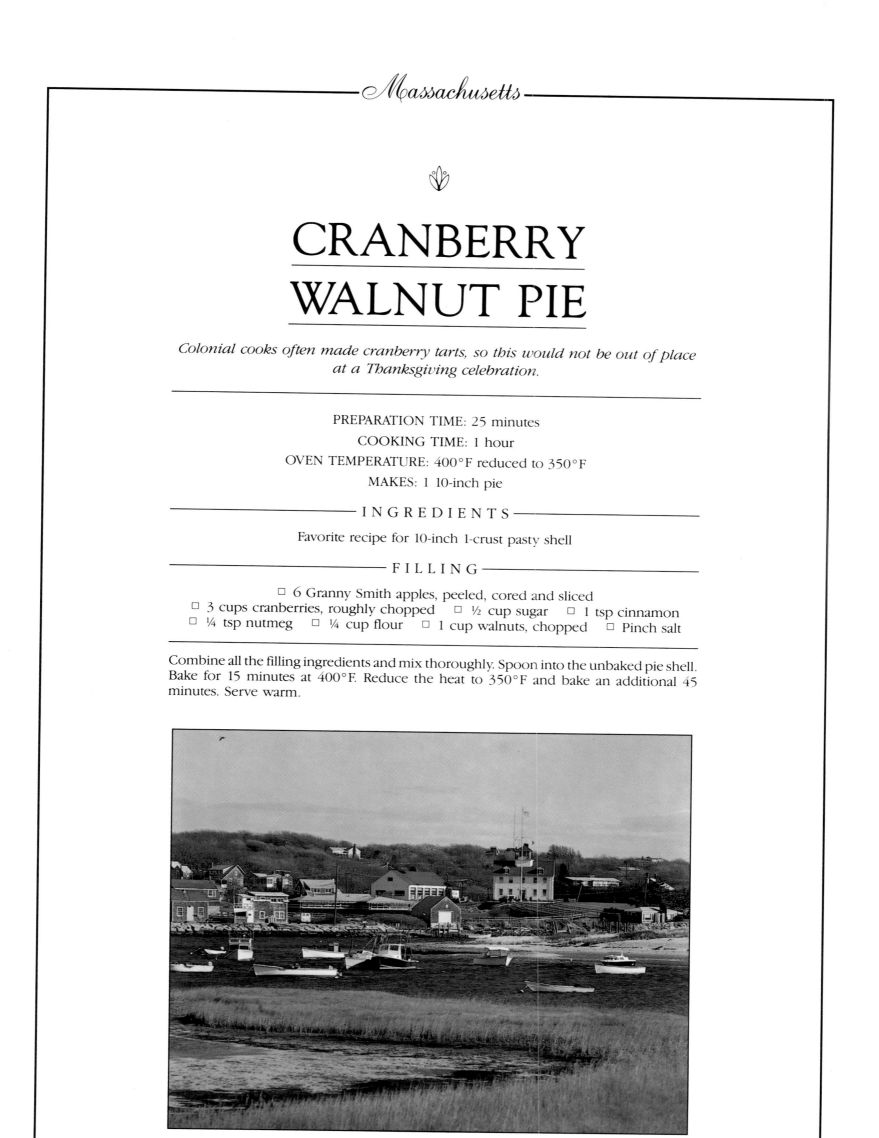

BERKSHIRE APPLE
PANCAKE

*These apple pancakes are similar to ones prepared in Germany
and also have something in common with the French fruit
and batter pudding called clafoutis.*

PREPARATION TIME: 30 minutes

COOKING TIME: 25-28 minutes

OVEN TEMPERATURE: 375°F reduced to 350°F

SERVES: 6

INGREDIENTS

□ 2½ cups all-purpose flour   □ 2oz shortening   □ 8 eggs
□ 1 pint buttermilk   □ 1¾ tsps salt   □ 1¾ tsps sugar
□ 1¾ tsps baking soda   □ 1½ tbsps baking powder   □ 1 tbsp vanilla extract
□ 1 tsp ground cinnamon   □ ⅛ tsp ground nutmeg   □ 2 tbsps melted butter
□ 2 large MacIntosh apples, peeled, cored and diced
□ 1 large MacIntosh apple, peeled, cored and sliced

GLAZE

□ 6oz pure maple syrup   □ 4 tbsps apple cider   □ 2 tbsps melted butter
□ ½ cup dark brown sugar

Combine all the dry ingredients and add the shortening, eggs, buttermilk, vanilla, cinnamon, nutmeg and melted butter. With a wooden spoon, mix all the ingredients together. Do not over-mix; the mixture should look lumpy. Add the 2 diced apples and fold into the mixture. Allow to stand for 15 minutes before cooking.

Meanwhile, make the glaze. Combine the butter and cider over a low heat and add the sugar, maple syrup and mix well. Lightly brush 6½ " French crêpe pans with softened butter. Heat in the oven for 3 minutes. Remove the pans from the oven and ladle in about 6 fl oz of the batter, bringing it to within a ¼ inch of the top of the pan. Decorate each pancake with 4 of the reserved apple slices. Return to the oven for a further 10 minutes. Reduce the heat to 350°F and bake for 15-18 minutes, or until a skewer comes out clean from the center when tested. Remove from the oven and allow to stand for 5 minutes. Loosen the pancake from the edges and slide out onto a warm plate. Lightly brush with glaze and serve the remaining glaze separately. Serve with fruit such as a strawberry fan or an orange twist, if desired. The pancake can also be prepared in one large skillet and sliced into wedges to serve.

CHEF STEPHEN MONGEON,
THE RED LION INN,
STOCKBRIDGE, MA

*Facing page: salt marshes such as these are a common sight along the Massachusetts coastline.
Above: Berkshire Apple Pancake.*

SHAKER-STYLE CHOCOLATE BREAD PUDDING WITH ENGLISH CREAM SAUCE

*The Shakers derived originally from a small branch of English Quakers.
There are few desserts more English than a bread pudding
with a custard sauce, so it is easy to understand how, far from home,
they found this dessert comforting.*

PREPARATION TIME: 20 minutes plus overnight
COOKING TIME: 1 hour
OVEN TEMPERATURE: 350°F
SERVES: 4-6

INGREDIENTS

PUDDING

□ 4 cups half and half   □ 3oz semi-sweet chocolate
□ 5 cups stale bread, cut in small dice   □ ¾ cup brown sugar
□ ½ tsp salt   □ 2 tsps vanilla extract   □ 1 cup ground walnuts
□ 1 cup seedless raisins   □ 5 eggs, beaten

SAUCE

□ 2 cups milk   □ 6 egg yolks   □ ⅓ cup sugar
□ 1 tsp vanilla extract

Place the half and half in a pan with the chocolate and heat until the chocolate is melted. Stir occasionally so that the chocolate melts evenly. Combine the bread with the sugar, salt, walnuts and raisins. Mix together, breaking up any lumps of brown sugar. Add the vanilla extract and the beaten eggs and mix together well. Add the hot chocolate mixture to the bread mixture and combine thoroughly. Pour into a well-greased 8″ tube pan. Place the tube pan in a larger deep pan and fill that pan with warm water until it comes halfway up the sides of the tube pan. Place the pudding in the oven for about 1 hour, or until set and firm. Test for doneness by inserting a knife into the pudding. If the blade comes out clean, the pudding is done. Let it cool, cover it and refrigerate for at least 12 hours. To unmold the pudding, let it stand in hot water for about 5 minutes and invert onto a serving platter.

Facing page: Shaker-Style Chocolate Bread Pudding with English Cream Sauce.

To prepare the sauce, place the yolks and the sugar together and whip with a wire whisk until they are pale yellow and form ribbons. Heat the milk and vanilla extract together and bring to the boil. Gradually add the milk to the egg mixture and combine well. Pour back into the pan and place over low heat. Cook the sauce until it thickens enough to coat the back of a spoon. While the sauce is cooking, stir it constantly and do not allow it to boil. Strain through a fine sieve into a serving dish and allow to cool to room temperature. Cover and place in the refrigerator until ready to use. The sauce is best served cold.

CHEF JAMES E. LOWE,
THE VILLAGE INN,
LENOX, MA

Flavor of
VERMONT

COUNTRY PÂTÉ

A scrumptious pork pâté prepared in the traditional way makes a wonderful first course and can be made two days ahead of time. The mixture can also be ground in a food processor, but don't over-work it; this pâté should be coarse-textured. Serve with French bread and cornichons.

PREPARATION TIME: 30 minutes

COOKING TIME: 4 hours

OVEN TEMPERATURE: 300°F

SERVES: 6

--- INGREDIENTS ---

☐ 1 pig's head (to yield 1½ lbs cooked meat, cleaned)
☐ 1¼ lbs pork liver   ☐ 2½ lbs fresh pork butt
☐ 2 medium onions   ☐ 1 carrot
☐ 2 cloves garlic   ☐ 2 tbsps butter
☐ Salt and white pepper

Purchase a cleaned pig's head from a butcher. Rinse it thoroughly and place in a large pot with enough water to cover. Add 1 of the onions and the carrot, peeled and chopped. Simmer until the meat is falling from the bones, at least 2 hours. Remove the meat from the pot and allow to cool. Remove meat from the bone and weigh out the 1½ lbs needed. Meanwhile, dice the liver and pork butt. Season with salt and pepper and refrigerate for 12 hours. Dice the remaining onion and garlic cloves and sauté in the butter. Combine with all the other prepared ingredients and run the mixture through a grinding machine on medium grinding plate. Place the ground mixture in a terrine with a tightly fitting cover. Bake, covered, for about 2½ hours. Refrigerate for 48 hours before serving.

NEW ENGLAND CULINARY INSTITUTE,
MONTPELIER, VT

Facing page: delicious Country Pâté is the sort of wholesome fare that complements the pastoral beauty of Vermont (above).

CABBAGE SOUP

An unusual combination, but one that uses everyday ingredients, readily available and simple to prepare. A pressure cooker will cut the cooking time by a third. This soup tastes even better when reheated the next day.

PREPARATION TIME: 25 minutes plus overnight soaking
COOKING TIME: 1 hour 50 minutes
SERVES: 4-6

INGREDIENTS

- □ 2 cups dried kidney beans
- □ 1 medium onion, thinly sliced
- □ 4 cloves garlic, chopped
- □ 3 tbsps duck or goose fat or butter
- □ 1 small cabbage, thinly sliced
- □ 2 tomatoes, peeled, seeded and chopped

Pick over and rinse the beans. Soak overnight in 2 quarts of cold water. In a heavy based pot, melt the fat or butter and cook the onion and cabbage slowly, stirring occasionally until translucent. Add the remaining ingredients, including the beans and soaking water. Bring to the boil and then simmer for 1½ hours or until the beans are tender. Check the seasoning and serve.

NEW ENGLAND CULINARY INSTITUTE,
MONTPELIER, VT

ROAST VERMONT TURKEY

Turkey is so closely associated with Thanksgiving that we often forget about cooking it at any other time. It's too good to limit to one day a year, and roasting a turkey is no more difficult than roasting a chicken. Try serving it with the recipe for Chestnut Stuffing.

PREPARATION TIME: 15 minutes
COOKING TIME: 3 hours
OVEN TEMPERATURE: 325°F
SERVES: 8-10

INGREDIENTS

- ☐ 1 fresh Vermont turkey, 20lbs in weight
- ☐ Salt and pepper
- ☐ 1 onion, peeled and quartered (optional)

Remove the giblets from the turkey and rinse thoroughly. Pat dry and season the cavity with salt and pepper. Place the turkey on a rack, breast side up, in a roasting pan. Cover the legs with foil and roast for 1-1½ hours in a preheated oven. Baste often. Remove the foil from the drumsticks and continue roasting for another 1½ hours or until the internal temperature at the thigh registers 180°F. Let rest for 20 minutes before carving. Add the onion to the roasting pan for the last 1½ hours, if desired, to give extra flavor to the gravy.

NEW ENGLAND CULINARY INSTITUTE,
MONTPELIER, VT

Facing page: a modern "frame" house in a woodland setting at Stowe. Above: the Mount Mansfield landscape transformed by a heavy fall of snow. Overleaf: (clockwise from back) Roast Vermont Turkey, Fresh Cranberry Sauce, Cabbage Soup, Chestnut Stuffing and Vermont Baked Beans.

FRESH CRANBERRY SAUCE

Cranberries are popular all over North America. Fresh berries do have their season, but good quality frozen ones are always available. Cranberry sauce is traditional with turkey, but try it with ham or pork, too.

PREPARATION TIME: 10 minutes

COOKING TIME: 10 minutes

SERVES: 4-6

INGREDIENTS

☐ 3 cups fresh or frozen whole cranberries
☐ 1 cup cane sugar   ☐ 1 cup water

Rinse and drain the fresh cranberries and pick over (omit rinsing if the berries are frozen). Mix the cup of sugar and water in a medium saucepan and heat gently until the sugar dissolves. Bring the mixture to the boil, stir and add the whole cranberries. Lower the heat immediately to a very slow boil. Cook the cranberries slowly, stirring occasionally, for about 10 minutes. Most of the berries will pop during this time. Take care not to burn. Remove from the heat and cool at room temperature in the saucepan or place in a heatproof bowl to cool. Refrigerate until ready to serve. Makes about 2 cups of fresh cranberry sauce.

NEW ENGLAND CULINARY INSTITUTE,
MONPELIER, VT

Facing page: ears of corn make an unusual decoration for the front door. Above: the village of Grafton has been completely renovated thanks to the inheritance money of Hall and Dean Mathey.

CHESTNUT STUFFING

Chestnuts make this bread stuffing rich and special. Dried chestnuts make it easy. Try the stuffing with game birds as well as with turkey and chicken for a pleasant change. If filling the bird with the stuffing mixture, do not fill until ready to roast.

PREPARATION TIME: 20 minutes plus overnight soaking

COOKING TIME: 1 hour and 10 minutes

SERVES: 8

INGREDIENTS

☐ 8oz dry chestnuts ☐ 8oz dry white bread
☐ 1 quart warm water ☐ 2 tsps salt
☐ 2 cups chicken stock ☐ 2 tbsps butter
☐ 4 tbsps onion, finely chopped ☐ 4 tbsps celery, finely chopped
☐ ½ tsp black pepper ☐ ¼ tsp poultry seasoning
☐ ¼ tsp sage ☐ 1 large egg

Cover the dry chestnuts with water and soak overnight. The next day, simmer the chestnuts in the soaking water for 2 hours until tender, but not mushy. Drain and cool the chestnuts, chop coarsely and set aside. Cube the bread and place in a large bowl. Soak in chicken stock and set aside. In a small skillet, sauté the onions and celery in the butter and add to the bread mixture. Add seasonings and stir in the egg. Add the chestnuts and mix well. Place the stuffing in a greased ovenproof pan, or use to fill a turkey, game bird or chicken. Cook in a moderately low oven for 1 hour.

NEW ENGLAND CULINARY INSTITUTE,
MONTPELIER, VT

Above: the gilded dome of the State Capitol in Montpelier is topped by a statue of Ceres, goddess of agriculture. Facing page: a tranquil scene by the Missiqui River.

VERMONT BAKED BEANS

What makes Vermont baked beans different from other versions? Maple syrup, of course! These beans take a long time to cook, but nothing this good ever came out of a can.

PREPARATION TIME: 30 minutes plus overnight soaking
COOKING TIME: 7-8 hours
OVEN TEMPERATURE: 325°F
SERVES: 8

INGREDIENTS

- □ 1 quart dried navy or yellow eye beans
- □ 4 slices bacon or ½ lb piece salt pork □ 1 medium onion, chopped
- □ ½ cup Vermont maple syrup □ 1 tsp dry mustard
- □ ½ tsp ginger □ ¼ tsp pepper
- □ 1 tsp salt

Pick over the beans, rinse with cold water and drain. Place the beans in a large pot and cover with about 4 quarts of cold water. Soak the beans overnight or at least 8 hours. After soaking, bring the pot of beans and water to the boil. Reduce the heat and simmer the beans about 1½ hours or until tender. Drain the beans and reserve the liquid. Place the beans in an ovenproof casserole or bean pot. Add the chopped onion and if using bacon, dice it before adding to the beans. Add reserved bean liquid to cover. Add the maple syrup and spices and mix thoroughly. If using salt pork instead of bacon, place on top of the beans. Bake the beans, covered, for 4-5 hours. Uncover, and cook another 3-4 hours, adding extra bean liquid, if necessary. May be prepared several days in advance and reheated.

NEW ENGLAND CULINARY INSTITUTE,
MONTPELIER, VT

CHANTERELLE OMELET

Chanterelles, those very French mushrooms, are also frequently found growing wild in wooded areas in Vermont. Avoid washing them, since they absorb water. Just wipe them with damp paper towels if cleaning is necessary. The omelet itself takes less than a minute to cook, so all the ingredients should be at hand before proceeding.

PREPARATION TIME: 15 minutes

COOKING TIME: 2-3 minutes

SERVES: 1

INGREDIENTS

☐ 2 tbsps butter   ☐ 3 eggs at room temperature
☐ 3oz fresh chanterelle mushrooms   ☐ 2 tbsps finely chopped parsley
☐ Salt and pepper

Slice the mushrooms and melt 1 tbsp of the butter in a small pan. Sauté the mushrooms quickly, season with salt and pepper and add the chopped parsley. Set aside and keep them warm. Beat the eggs thoroughly with a fork or whisk in a small bowl. Place the remaining butter in an omelet pan and heat until foaming but not brown. Pour in the eggs and swirl over the bottom of the pan. Immediately stir the eggs with a fork to allow the uncooked mixture to fall to the bottom of the pan. When the mixture is creamily set on top, scatter over the sautéed chanterelles and roll the omelet in the pan by flipping about a third of it to the middle and then flipping it out onto a hot plate.

NEW ENGLAND CULINARY INSTITUTE,
MONTPELIER, VT

Above: the golden glow of a fall afternoon in Vermont. Facing page: wild mushrooms are one of fall's tastiest crops — Chanterelle Omelet makes the most of them.

SUCCOTASH

Succotash is an Indian name for a dish of corn and beans. Sometimes, the only beans used are lima beans. The addition of red peppers makes a trio of appetizing colors. Serve as a side dish with meat or poultry.

PREPARATION TIME: 25 minutes

COOKING TIME: 15 minutes

SERVES: 6

INGREDIENTS

☐ 2oz butter   ☐ 2 cups cooked fresh kernel corn
☐ 2 cups cooked fresh lima beans   ☐ 2 cups cooked fresh green beans
☐ 1 red pepper, seeded and thinly sliced   ☐ 1 tsp salt
☐ ¼ tsp white pepper

Melt the butter in a saucepan and add the cooked vegetables, salt and pepper to taste. Heat the succotash over low heat, tossing occasionally. Pour into a serving dish and decorate with the red pepper slices.

NEW ENGLAND CULINARY INSTITUTE,
MONTPELIER, VT

VERMONT
COB-SMOKED HAM

*Not all hams are the same. Cob smoking gives the Vermont ham
a unique and very pleasant taste. Some Vermonters
like to baste the ham with fresh apple cider during the last
30 minutes of cooking. Plan to serve 3 people with each 1lb of ham.*

PREPARATION TIME: 10 minutes

COOKING TIME: 12 minutes per lb

OVEN TEMPERATURE: 300°F

SERVES: 3 people per lb

— INGREDIENTS —

☐ 1 Vermont cob-smoked ham   ☐ Fresh apple cider (optional)

Place the Vermont ham in a large roasting pan and insert a meat thermometer into the
thickest part, avoiding the bone. Bake the ham, uncovered, for 12 minutes per lb. When
done, the ham will have an internal temperature of 120°F.

NEW ENGLAND CULINARY INSTITUTE,
MONTPELIER, VT

*Facing page: Succotash and Vermont Cob-Smoked Ham. Above: isolated farmhouses are a common sight
in a state where sixty-six per cent of the population lives in rural locations.*

TRUITE AU BLEU

The French influence is at work in this recipe. It is, of course, only the skin of the trout which turns blue when cooked by this method. Success depends on using very fresh fish and minimal handling to preserve the natural slime on the fish skin.

PREPARATION TIME: 30 minutes

COOKING TIME: 40 minutes

SERVES: 4

INGREDIENTS

□ 4 live trout   □ 24 live crawfish
□ ⅓ cup red wine vinegar   □ 1 small onion, peeled and sliced
□ 1 small carrot, peeled and sliced   □ ½ a lemon, sliced
□ 2 sprigs fresh thyme   □ 2 tsps salt
□ Melted butter for serving

Combine all the ingredients except the fish and melted butter in a large pot and add 1 quart of water to make a court bouillon. Simmer for 30 minutes and allow to cool. Kill the trout by hitting it on the head once sharply with a heavy object. With a sharp knife, eviscerate the fish. Place the trout and crawfish into the court bouillon. Bring back to the boil and allow to simmer. Turn off the heat and let stand 10 minutes before removing the trout and crawfish to a heated platter for serving. Serve with melted butter.

NEW ENGLAND CULINARY INSTITUTE,
MONTPELIER, VT

Facing page: Truite au Bleu. Above: Vermont's state tree is the sugar maple, at its most splendid in fall.

VENISON STEW

Vermont has more deer per land area than any other state, so hunting is popular and recipes for venison are abundant. In the 19th century, many French Canadians from Quebec settled in Vermont and their culinary influence is evident in dishes like this, reminiscent of French country stews.

PREPARATION TIME: 30 minutes plus overnight marinating

COOKING TIME: 1½ hours

SERVES: 6-8

———————————— I N G R E D I E N T S ————————————

◻ 6lbs boneless venison shoulder, cubed
◻ 1 quart good quality red wine   ◻ ¼ cup red wine vinegar
◻ 1 bay leaf   ◻ 2 sprigs of fresh thyme
◻ 6 juniper berries   ◻ 1 medium carrot, peeled and cut into ¼ inch dice
◻ 1 medium onion, peeled and cut into ¼ inch dice
◻ 2 celery sticks, cut into ¼ inch dice
◻ 4 cloves garlic, crushed   ◻ ½ cup vegetable oil
◻ ½ cup flour   ◻ 1lb mushrooms, quartered
◻ 1lb slab bacon, cut in ½ inch pieces   ◻ Pinch salt and pepper

Combine the wine, vinegar, carrot, onion and celery and marinate with the cubed venison for 24 hours. Remove the meat and vegetables from the marinade and place in separate bowls. Reserve the marinade. Heat the oil in a heavy frying pan and brown the venison on all sides over high heat. Remove the venison from the frying pan to a large pot, repeat the browning process with the vegetables and add to the venison in a large pot. Sprinkle the flour over the combined meat and vegetables, stir and add the reserved marinade. Add salt and pepper to taste. Simmer for about 1 hour, remove the vegetables after that time and reserve them. Continue cooking the meat until tender, about 1½ hours. Meanwhile, blanch the bacon for 3 minutes in boiling water. Drain and sauté in the same skillet used for the venison. Add the bacon to the stew when the venison is tender. Sauté the mushrooms and add to the stew. Cook until all the ingredients are hot and serve immediately. A chesnut purée makes a nice accompaniment.

NEW ENGLAND CULINARY INSTITUTE,
MONTPELIER, VT

Facing page: Venison Stew.

ROAST LOIN
OF PORK

In early New England, pork was more plentiful than beef and the colonists frequently made use of this delicious meat. Pork loin used to be cooked with the crackling left on, as it is in England, but this is now out of fashion. Be sure to have the backbone and feather bone split to make carving easier.

PREPARATION TIME: 20 minutes

COOKING TIME: 40 minutes per lb

OVEN TEMPERATURE: 450°F reduced to 325°F

—— INGREDIENTS ——

- 1 pork loin roast – 2 ribs per person
- 3 large onions
- Sage
- Thyme
- Salt and pepper

Remove the roast from the refrigerator about 1 hour before cooking. Preheat the oven to 450°F. Rub the sage, thyme, salt and pepper onto all sides of the pork loin. Cover the ends of the bones with foil to protect them from burning. Slice the onions and place the pork on top of them in an ovenproof dish. Place the roast in the oven and reduce the heat to 325°F. Cook 40 minutes to the pound, basting often with the pan juices. Allow to rest for 15 minutes before carving. Accompany with Three Cabbages recipe.

NEW ENGLAND CULINARY INSTITUTE,
MONTPELIER, VT

THREE CABBAGES

Serve this dish with roast loin of pork for a combination that is popular in so many countries. In the true melting pot spirit of America, this recipe takes the sauerkraut of Germany, Savoy cabbage of England and red cabbage of Denmark and brings them together in one special dish. While the recipe is prepared in three separate sections, the cabbages are ultimately served together as one dish.

PREPARATION TIME: 35 minutes

COOKING TIME: 1½ hours

SERVES: 6-8

INGREDIENTS

SAUERKRAUT

☐ 1 medium onion, sliced ☐ 2lbs fresh sauerkraut (unrinsed)
☐ 1 cup white wine ☐ 6 juniper berries
☐ 6oz slab bacon ☐ White pepper to taste

SAVOY CABBAGE

☐ 1 large Savoy cabbage, sliced thinly ☐ 3 tbsps butter
☐ Salt and pepper

RED CABBAGE

☐ 1 large red cabbage, sliced thinly ☐ 1 cup red wine
☐ ½ cup red wine vinegar ☐ 1 tsp salt
☐ ¼ cup sugar ☐ ½ tsp thyme
☐ ½ cup water ☐ ¼ cup oil
☐ 1 onion, thinly sliced

Melt the butter for the sauerkraut in a heavy saucepan and add the onion. Cook the onion slowly until it is transparent, not brown. Add the remaining ingredients and simmer 1 hour. Set aside.

Bring 2 gallons of water to the boiling point. Drop in the Savoy cabbage and cook for 2 minutes. Remove from the heat and cool immediately. Drain the cabbage well. Melt the butter and place in a bowl with the cooked Savoy cabbage. Toss, season and set aside.

Combine the red cabbage, wine, vinegar, salt, sugar, water and thyme and marinate the mixture in the refrigerator. Drain, reserving the liquid. In a heavy saucepan, heat the oil and sweat the onion slowly. Add the drained cabbage and stir. Add the reserved liquid and cook, covered, for 1½ hours. Remove the cover and cook the cabbage until the liquid is almost evaporated. Reheat the Savoy cabbage and arrange all three cabbages attractively together and serve with roast pork.

NEW ENGLAND CULINARY INSTITUTE,
MONTPELIER, VT

Facing page: the stark outlines of silos are a familiar sight in the lush farmlands of Vermont.
Overleaf: Three Cabbages, Roast Loin of Pork, Upside-Down Apple Pie and Lattice Apple Pie.

UPSIDE-DOWN
APPLE PIE

Many Vermont recipes have French counterparts and the origin of this one can be seen in the famous Tarte Tatin. When turned out, this pie looks so impressive you will be amazed that it was so easy to prepare.

PREPARATION TIME: 25 minutes

COOKING TIME: 40 minutes

OVEN TEMPERATURE: 400°F

SERVES: 6-8

INGREDIENTS

□ 12 Golden Delicious apples   □ 6-8oz butter
□ 1 cup sugar   □ Rind of 1 lemon
□ Recipe for your favorite one-crust pastry

Peel, seed and cut each apple into 6 wedges. In a frying pan, place 3-4oz butter and half the sugar. Cook on low heat, stirring occasionally, until the mixture reaches a light caramel color. Add the apples in small batches and cook until they are tender, but still holding their shape. Set aside and repeat with the remaining apples until all are cooked. In another small frying pan, place 3-4oz butter and melt until foaming. Add the remaining sugar and the lemon rind and cook until light caramel in color. Allow to cool. Pour the light caramel mixture into a large pie plate. Arrange the apple wedges side-by-side until the caramel is covered and all the apples are used. Make two layers of apples. Roll the dough and place on top of the apples. Trim the crust so that it comes to the edge of the apples. Bake for 40 minutes. Run a knife around the edge to loosen the crust and let the pie stand for 10 minutes. Place a large serving plate on top of the pan and invert the pie onto the serving dish. Serve with whipped cream.

NEW ENGLAND CULINARY INSTITUTE,
MONTPELIER, VT

Facing page: once the Vermont winter begins to set in, a good stack of logs for the grate is essential. Above: as the snows melt, streams and rivers swell.

LATTICE APPLE PIE

The use of apple cider in this pie is characteristic of Vermont cooking. Taste the apples first to decide how much sugar to add and use white or light brown, as desired. Grating over some maple sugar is a delicious idea, too.

PREPARATION TIME: 35 minutes
COOKING TIME: 45 minutes
OVEN TEMPERATURE: 450°F reducing to 350°F
MAKES: 1 pie

INGREDIENTS

☐ Use your favorite two-crust pastry recipe

FILLING

☐ 6 cups apples, peeled and thinly sliced
(Northern Spy apples are good)
☐ 1 tsp cinnamon ☐ ½ tsp nutmeg
☐ 1 tbsp butter ☐ 2 tbsps apple cider

Line a 9-inch pie dish with half the pastry. It is not necessary to grease the pie dish since the pastry has a high fat content. Place a layer of apples on top of the pastry, scattering sugar and spices over. Repeat with the remaining apples and the sugar and spices until the dish is full. Dot the top layer with small pieces of butter and sprinkle on the apple cider. Moisten the edge of the bottom crust with a damp (not wet) pastry brush. For the top, roll out the remaining pastry and cut into strips. Place the strips on top of the apples in a criss-cross design. If a glaze is desired, brush with beaten egg mixed with a pinch of salt. Bake the pie for 15 minutes in a 450°F oven. Reduce the heat to 350°F and continue cooking for approximately 30 minutes longer, until the lattice is browned and the apples are tender.

NEW ENGLAND CULINARY INSTITUTE,
MONTPELIER, VT

Above: those distant slopes become a skiers' paradise in winter, while water sports enthusiasts are served by Vermont's numerous lakes (facing page).

PUMPKIN
CHEESECAKE

An interesting way of using pumpkin is to combine it with cream cheese in a deliciously rich cheesecake. Try it as an alternative to pumpkin pie for Thanksgiving dinner.

PREPARATION TIME: 20 minutes

COOKING TIME: 1 hour 50 minutes

OVEN TEMPERATURE: 325°F

MAKES: 1 cake

INGREDIENTS

CHEESECAKE CRUST

- ☐ 1 cup graham cracker crumbs
- ☐ ¼ cup brown sugar
- ☐ ½ cup melted butter or margarine

PUMPKIN FILLING

- ☐ 4 8oz packages cream cheese, softened
- ☐ 1 cup granulated sugar
- ☐ ½ cup brown sugar, packed
- ☐ 5 eggs, beaten
- ☐ 2 cups canned pumpkin
- ☐ 2 tsps pumpkin pie spice
- ☐ 1 tsp vanilla

DECORATION

- ☐ Whipped cream
- ☐ Cherries
- ☐ Walnuts
- ☐ Fresh mint

Combine the ingredients for the cheesecake crust and mix well. Press into a 9 inch spring-form pan and bake for 8-10 minutes at 425°F. Place the cream cheese in a mixing bowl and beat in the sugar until the mixture is light and fluffy. Add the beaten eggs gradually and mix in the remaining ingredients. Pour on top of the crust in the spring-form pan and lower the oven temperature to 325°F. Bake for 1 hour 20 minutes, or until the cake is firm around the edges. Turn off the heat and let the cake remain in the oven an additional 30 minutes. Cool on a rack completely before removing from the tin. Garnish the top with whipped cream, cherries, walnuts and fresh mint leaves.

BERNADETTE CHOUINARD,
DANVILLE, VT

Facing page: Pumpkin Cheesecake uses a familiar ingredient in an innovative way.

MAPLE WALNUT BREAD

One whole cup of maple syrup gives a true Vermont taste to this quick bread. The orange juice adds a fresh tang. This bread is better if 'ripened' for at least one day before eating.

PREPARATION TIME: 20 minutes

COOKING TIME: 1 hour

OVEN TEMPERATURE: 250°F

MAKES: 1 loaf

INGREDIENTS

☐ 2 tbsps melted butter ☐ 1 cup Vermont maple syrup
☐ 1 egg, well beaten ☐ Grated rind of 1 lemon
☐ 2½ cups flour ☐ 3 tsps baking powder
☐ ½ tsp baking soda ☐ ¼ tsp salt
☐ ¾ cup walnuts, chopped (3 reserved whole for decoration)
☐ ¾ cup orange juice

Blend the butter, maple syrup, egg and lemon rind until creamy. In a separate bowl, sift the dry ingredients together and add the nuts. Combine the two mixtures alternately with the orange juice. Bake in a greased loaf pan in a moderate oven for 1 hour. After the bread cools, glaze with more maple syrup and put the reserved walnuts on top. Best served the day after baking.

NEW ENGLAND CULINARY INSTITUTE,
MONTPELIER, VT

Facing page: maple syrup is first extracted from the trees as sap and then reduced in wooden sugarhouses, such as this one at Johnson. Overleaf (from back): Maple Walnut Bread, Maple Mousse, Maple Baked Apples and Acorn Squash with Maple and Prunes all use this famous syrup.

MAPLE MOUSSE

Refined from the sap of the sugar maple tree, maple is the finest of all syrups.
Don't be tempted to use substitutes in this rich mousse;
that would never be Vermont style!

PREPARATION TIME: 30 minutes

COOKING TIME: 10 minutes

SERVES: 6

INGREDIENTS

□ 6 egg yolks □ 1 cup Grade A Vermont maple syrup
□ 1½ cups heavy cream

In a saucepan, bring the maple syrup to the boiling point and cook rapidly to reduce from 1 cup to ¾ cup. Be careful not to let the syrup burn. Meanwhile, in a stainless steel bowl, whip the egg yolks until foamy. Pour in the reduced maple syrup slowly over the beaten egg yolks, whipping constantly. Continue whipping the mixture until cool. In a separate bowl, whip the heavy cream until stiff. Fold the cream gently into the mousse mixture and pour into a chilled bowl. Refrigerate until set and serve chilled.

NEW ENGLAND CULINARY INSTITUTE,
MONTPELIER, VT

Green and gold are the colors most associated with Vermont, whether in lush landscapes (above)
or in hazy fall sunsets (facing page).

MAPLE BAKED APPLES

Maple syrup, for which Vermont is justly famous, finds its way into many of the state's outstanding recipes. Syrup in this recipe helps to make a delicious sauce for the baked apples.

PREPARATION TIME: 5 minutes
COOKING TIME: 35-40 minutes
OVEN TEMPERATURE: 325°F
SERVES: 6

INGREDIENTS

- 6 baking apples (Rome, Baldwin, Cortland, Greenings, McIntosh or Golden Delicious)
- 6oz unsalted butter   □ ¾ cup Vermont maple syrup
- ¼ tsp mace   □ Juice of 1 lemon

Wash and core the apples and place them in a lightly greased ovenproof dish. Combine the butter, maple syrup, mace and lemon juice in a saucepan and bring to the boil. Pour the mixture over the apples. Place the dish of apples in a preheated oven and bake for 35-40 minutes. Baste the apples often with the maple mixture. The apples are done when they soften and look shiny.

NEW ENGLAND CULINARY INSTITUTE,
MONTPELIER, VT

ACORN SQUASH WITH MAPLE AND PRUNES

Squash was one of the first vegetables the early settlers learned to grow. However, the many different varieties available now would have bewildered our forefathers. Acorn squash is a winter variety and the rind should be very hard for the vegetable to be good.

PREPARATION TIME: 25 minutes

COOKING TIME: 32-38 minutes

OVEN TEMPERATURE: 325°F

SERVES: 6

————————————— I N G R E D I E N T S —————————————

□ 3 medium acorn squash   □ 12 pitted prunes
□ ¾ cup Vermont maple syrup   □ 3oz butter
□ Salt to taste

Split the acorn squash horizontally with a sharp knife and remove the seeds. Blanch or parboil in salted water for 7-8 minutes. Remove the squash and place cavity side up in an ovenproof baking dish. Place 2 prunes in the cavity of the squash half, along with 2 tbsps of maple syrup, a pat of butter and a pinch of salt. Bake the squash in a preheated oven for 25-30 minutes, basting occasionally. Serve as a side dish with pork or poultry.

NEW ENGLAND CULINARY INSTITUTE,
MONTPELIER, VT

Facing page: snow begins to transform the landscape even before the last of the leaves have fallen.

PUMPKIN PIE

In the 18th century this pie would have been called a pudding. Spices were not included, though, until the clipper ships began their trade. In the Southern states, squash is often used as an alternative ingredient, but whichever you choose, Thanksgiving would not be the same without it.

PREPARATION TIME: 25 minutes

COOKING TIME: 45 minutes

OVEN TEMPERATURE: 400°F

MAKES: 1 pie

INGREDIENTS

☐ 1½ cups cooked and mashed pumpkin ☐ 2 eggs
☐ 1 cup milk ☐ ½ cup brown sugar
☐ 1 tsp cinnamon ☐ ½ tsp ginger
☐ ¼ tsp nutmeg ☐ Recipe for one-crust pastry, baked until very pale brown

Place all the ingredients, except the eggs and pastry, into the top of a double boiler. Over boiling water, bring the mixture just to the scalding point. In a bowl, beat the eggs until frothy. Stir a small amount of the hot mixture into the eggs and return the egg mixture to the rest of the hot pumpkin. Stir over heat continuously until the mixture begins to thicken. Pour into the baked pie shell. Bake the pumpkin pie until the filling sets and a knife tip inserted into the center of the filling comes out clean, about 30 minutes. Serve slightly warm with whipped cream.

NEW ENGLAND CULINARY INSTITUTE,
MONTPELIER, VT

Facing page: pumpkins are as important a part of Halloween as of Thanksgiving celebrations. Above: starkly silhouetted hills enhance the drama of this sunset over Lake Champlain.

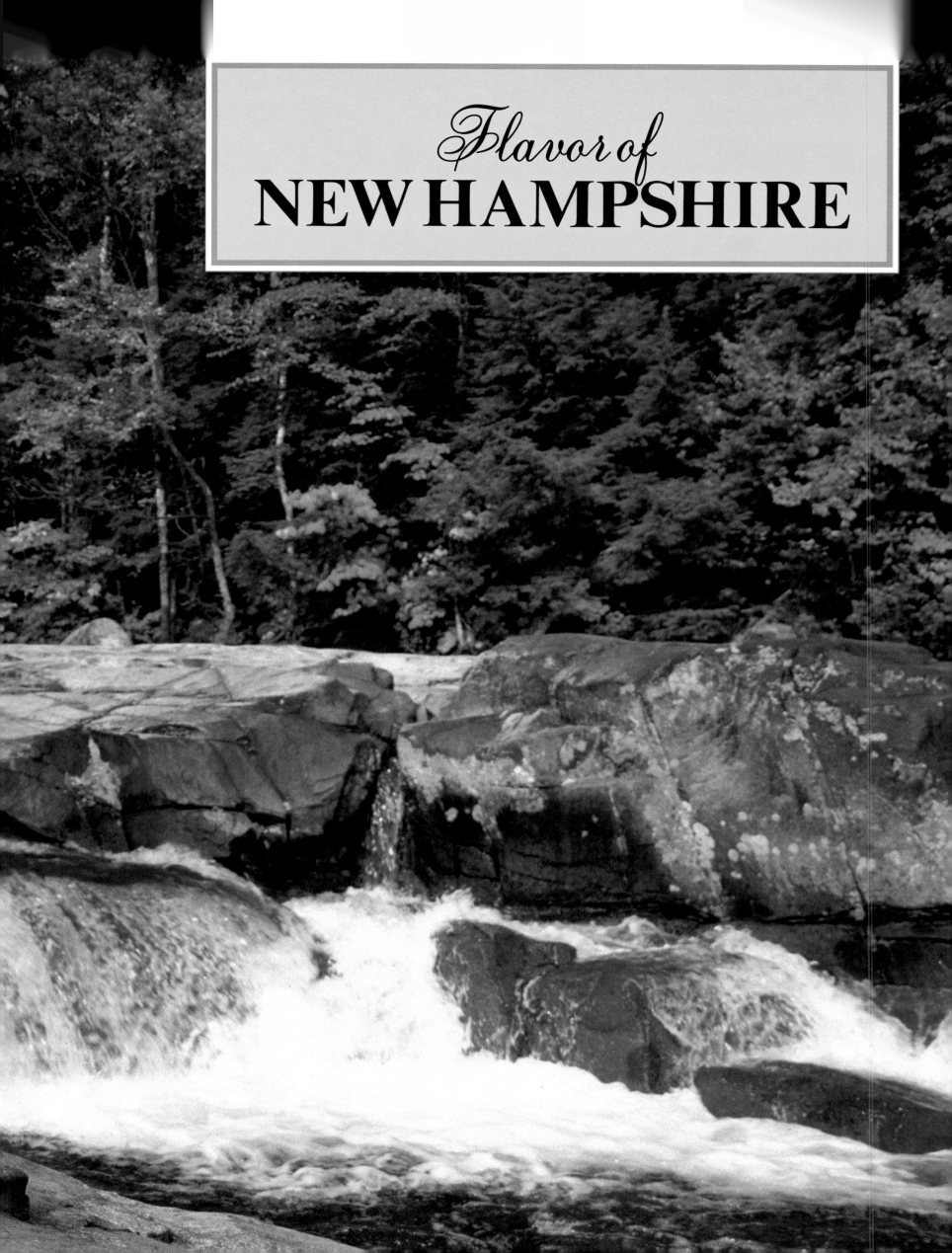

Flavor of
NEW HAMPSHIRE

CRUDITÉ VEGETABLE PRESENTATION WITH NEW HAMPSHIRE HORSERADISH AND GARLIC DIP

Raw vegetables with dips are easy to prepare and serve and they add a splash of color to an hors d'oeuvre selection. Using a cabbage to hold the dip is a whimsical touch, and you can eat the dish!

PREPARATION TIME: 40 minutes plus overnight chilling
SERVES: 8-10

Previous pages: the aptly named Swift River flows through the Rocky Gorge Scenic Area, near Passaconaway. Above: Crudité Vegetable Presentation with New Hampshire Horseradish and Garlic Dip.

INGREDIENTS

- □ ½ lb broccoli flowerets, washed   □ ¼ lb cauliflower flowerets, washed
- □ ¼ lb julienne strips of carrot and celery
- □ 4 asparagus tips, cut into 3-inch lengths
- □ 4 radish rosettes   □ 8 sprigs fresh parsley
- □ 1 head red kale or Savoy cabbage

DIP

- □ 6oz fresh dairy sour cream   □ 1 tbsp minced fresh garlic
- □ 1 tbsp minced fresh horseradish   □ ½ tsp white pepper
- □ ½ tsp sea salt   □ ¼ tsp dry mustard
- □ 1 tsp cognac

Blend all the dip ingredients together and chill 24 hours. Make the radish rosettes and clean and trim the vegetables. Hollow out a space in the cabbage deep enough to hold the dip, fill and place in the middle of an attractive serving dish. Arrange all the vegetables around the cabbage to serve.

GREGORY MARTIN,
WHITE RABBIT CATERING,
HOOKSETT, NH

*Above: the lakes region of New Hampshire is made up of over a hundred lakes
and is a favorite spot for those in search of an active outdoor vacation.*

CHARTREUSE OF VEGETABLES

A chartreuse in French cooking is a molded dish that has one main ingredient complemented by smaller quantities of choicer ingredients, in this case, fluffy mashed potatoes with a selection of colorful garden vegetables. Be generous with the quantity of mashed potatoes because this is what holds the dish together. Don't be afraid to try it; it only looks complicated.

PREPARATION TIME: 40 minutes

COOKING TIME: 25 minutes

OVEN TEMPERATURE: 425°F

SERVES: 6-8

INGREDIENTS

- Potatoes, peeled and cubed
- Carrots, cut in julienne strips
- String beans, trimmed
- Peas
- Zucchini
- Summer squash
- Cabbage leaves
- Brussels sprouts
- Cauliflower flowerets

Cook the potatoes about 20 minutes and drain them well. Dry over heat while mashing. Trim the carrot sticks and string beans to fit the height of a soufflé dish. Slice the zucchini and summer squash, trim down thick ribs of the cabbage leaves and trim the ends of the Brussels sprouts. Parboil all the vegetables for about 2 minutes. Drain and rinse under cold water and leave to dry. Butter a soufflé dish thickly. Arrange a row of peas along the edge of the bottom of the dish. Next to the peas arrange a row of sliced zucchini and then fill in the center with circles of summer squash. Line the sides of the dish with carrot sticks and string beans, alternating the two. Butter will hold the vegetables in place. Carefully spread a layer of mashed potato over the bottom and up the sides to completely cover the carrots and beans. Add a thick layer to hold the vegetables together. Place a cabbage leaf or two on top of the potatoes and press gently to firm the vegetables. On the cabbage make a circle of Brussels sprouts around the outside edge and fill in the center with cauliflower. On top of that arrange another circle of zucchini and summer squash. Top with a cabbage leaf and fill with more mashed potatoes, smoothing the top. Bake in a preheated 425°F oven for 20 minutes. Remove from the oven and allow to set for 3-5 minutes before inverting onto a serving dish. If necessary, loosen the sides of the chartreuse from the dish with a sharp knife before turning out.

JAMES HALLER'S KITCHEN,
26 LIBERTY STREET,
SOUTH BERWICK,
MAINE
(FORMERLY OF PORTSMOUTH, NH)

Facing page: this artfully presented Chartreuse of Vegetables is a colorful reinterpretation of a classic dish.

NEW HAMPSHIRE MAPLE BAKED BEANS WITH BOURBON

*Baked beans are popular all over New England and each
state has its own versions. The secret ingredients in this recipe are New
Hampshire's own maple syrup, bourbon and, surprisingly, coffee.*

PREPARATION TIME: 15 minutes plus overnight soaking

COOKING TIME: 9 hours

OVEN TEMPERATURE: 250°F

SERVES: 8-10

INGREDIENTS

☐ 1 cup pea beans (soaked overnight)
☐ 2 tsps dry mustard ☐ ½ tsp freshly ground pepper
☐ ¼ tsps ground ginger ☐ 3 tsps white vinegar
☐ 3 tsps malt vinegar ☐ 1½ cups strongly brewed coffee
☐ ¾ cup New Hampshire maple syrup ☐ 1¼ tsps dark molasses
☐ 1 large onion, finely chopped ☐ ¾ lb salt pork
☐ ¾ cup Jim Beam Kentucky Straight Bourbon

Drain the beans and set aside. In a large bowl, combine mustard, pepper, ginger, vinegars
and coffee. Add maple syrup and molasses and mix well. Add the onion and pork. Pour
in the bourbon and stir in the beans. Transfer to an oven-proof baking dish, if necessary,
and bake overnight (about 9 hours) in a preheated oven. It may be necessary to add water
several times during cooking, so that the beans do not dry out.

GREGORY MARTIN,
WHITE RABBIT CATERING,
HOOKSETT, NH

FRESH CREAMED MUSHROOMS

For a recipe that has been around since Colonial times, this one is surprisingly up-to-date.

PREPARATION TIME: 20 minutes

COOKING TIME: 7 minutes

SERVES: 4

INGREDIENTS

☐ 1lb even-sized button mushrooms   ☐ 1 tbsp lemon juice
☐ 2 tbsps butter or margarine   ☐ 1 tbsp flour   ☐ Salt and white pepper
☐ ¼ tsp freshly grated nutmeg   ☐ 1 small bay leaf   ☐ 1 blade mace
☐ 1 cup heavy cream   ☐ 1 tbsp dry sherry

Wash the mushrooms quickly and dry them well. Trim the stems level with the caps. Leave whole if small, halve or quarter if large. Toss with the lemon juice and set aside. In a medium saucepan, melt the butter or margarine and stir in the flour. Cook, stirring gently, for about 1 minute. Remove from the heat, add the nutmeg, salt, pepper, bay leaf and mace and gradually stir in the cream. Return the pan to the heat and bring to the boil, stirring constantly. Allow to boil for about 1 minute, or until thickened. Reduce the heat and add the mushrooms. Simmer gently, covered, for about 5 minutes, or until the mushrooms are tender. Add the sherry during the last few minutes of cooking. Remove bay leaf and blade mace. Sprinkle with additional grated nutmeg before serving.

Facing page: New Hampshire Maple Baked Beans with Bourbon. Above: Fresh Creamed Mushrooms.

CRANBERRY DUCK L' ORANGE

Indians were the first to use cranberries to brighten up food. The beautiful bright red color of these berries adds verve and their tangy, fresh taste is the perfect complement to the richness of duck.

PREPARATION TIME: 20 minutes
COOKING TIME: 1½ hours
OVEN TEMPERATURE: 350°F
SERVES: 2

INGREDIENTS

- □ 1 duck, about 4lbs in weight
- □ 1 tbsp ground sage
- □ 1 tbsp ground black pepper
- □ 1 tsp thyme
- □ 1 tsp nutmeg
- □ Rind of 1 orange, grated
- □ 3 tbsps ground cranberries
- □ 2 tbsps olive oil
- □ 2 tbsps salt
- □ 3 tbsps orange juice

Wash the duck and dry it well. Combine all the other ingredients and mix well. The cranberries can be ground in a food processor if desired. Rub the duck inside and outside with the mixture. Place seasoned duck on a rack in a deep roasting pan. Line the pan with foil for easier clean-up. Cover the duck loosely with foil and roast in a preheated oven for 1½ hours, or until juices run clear when the thickest part of the thigh is pierced with a skewer. Serve with cranberry relish.

GREGORY MARTIN,
WHITE RABBIT CATERING,
HOOKSETT, NH

Above: New Hampshire's fall colors are reflected in Cranberry Duck L'Orange and Cranberry Bog Relish (facing page). Also in the picture are Red Bliss Potato Salad, and Gregory's Golden Puffs with New Hampshire Shrimp Mousse.

GREGORY'S GOLDEN PUFFS WITH NEW HAMPSHIRE SHRIMP MOUSSE

Choux pastry puffs make elegant hors d'oeuvres. Shape them small to serve with drinks, or larger for a first course. New Hampshire shrimp and Cheddar cheese make these especially good.

PREPARATION TIME: 25 minutes

COOKING TIME: 40 minutes

OVEN TEMPERATURE: 420°F reduced to 250°F

MAKES: about 24 puffs

— INGREDIENTS —

— PUFFS —

☐ 1 cup water   ☐ 4oz butter
☐ 1 cup bread flour   ☐ 5 eggs

Above: calm and serene, Echo Lake, near North Conway, is fringed by trees and dominated by rocky crags.

MOUSSE

- □ 1lb fresh cooked New Hampshire shrimp
- □ 4oz New Hampshire Cheddar cheese
- □ 2 tbsps minced fresh garlic □ 6oz farm fresh sour cream
- □ ½ tsp salt □ ½ tsp white pepper
- □ ½ tsp dry vermouth □ ½ tsp Helmet mustard, ground
- □ 1oz Danish blue cheese

To prepare the puffs, bring the water and butter to the boil in a heavy pan. Once boiling, sift in the cup of flour and stir over very low heat with a whisk. Once the mixture comes away from the sides of the pan, beat in the eggs, one at a time. Continue beating in the eggs over low heat until the mixture is smooth and shiny – it may not be necessary to add all the eggs. Transfer the pastry into a pastry bag fitted with a large plain tip. Pipe the mixture out onto a greased baking sheet in amounts about 2 inches tall and equally wide. Alternatively, pipe out in decorative shapes such as little turbans or simple round mounds. Place in a preheated oven for 30 minutes. Reduce the heat to 250°F for 10 minutes longer, or until the puffs are golden brown and crisp. Remove from the oven and, using a sharp skewer, pierce a hole the size of a small plain piping tip in the bottom. Allow to cool completely while preparing the mousse.

In a food processor, combine all the mousse ingredients and blend until smooth. When the puffs are completely cold, fill a pastry bag fitted with a plain tip with the mousse mixture and pipe through the prepared holes in the puffs. Do not fill the puffs more than 30 minutes before serving.

GREGORY MARTIN,
WHITE RABBIT CATERING,
HOOKSETT, NH

*Above: the 724,000-square-acre White Mountain National Forest
covers most of north-central New Hampshire.*

FRESH CRANBERRY
BOG RELISH

Once the Pilgrims were introduced to cranberries, they made frequent use of them in sauces and relishes to accompany meats, poultry and game. The addition of lemon and lime in this relish adds a fresh twist to an old American classic.

PREPARATION TIME: 5-10 minutes

MAKES: about 4 cups

INGREDIENTS

☐ 2 cups fresh whole cranberries   ☐ 2 cups granulated sugar
☐ ½ fresh lemon, cut into quarters   ☐ ½ fresh orange, cut into quarters
☐ ½ fresh lime, cut into quarters   ☐ ¼ tsp nutmeg
☐ ¼ tsp cinnamon

Combine all the ingredients in a food processor to blend 2 minutes or until finely ground. Place in a saucepan and cook over medium heat for about 1 hour or until thick and bubbling. Stir frequently and add water if necessary to prevent drying out and burning. Serve with poultry, game, pork or ham.

GREGORY MARTIN,
WHITE RABBIT CATERING,
HOOKSETT, NH

Above: the State Capitol Building in Concord is the nation's oldest in which the legislature still sits in its original chambers.

RED BLISS
POTATO SALAD

Most of the goodness in a potato is in its skin. That is why potatoes, except if they are old and very thick-skinned, should not be peeled before they are cooked. Serve them in their skins too, whenever possible. Using red potatoes adds extra color and interest to the dish.

PREPARATION TIME: 20 minutes

COOKING TIME: 20-30 minutes

SERVES: 8

— INGREDIENTS —

□ 3 lbs Red Bliss potatoes   □ 2 tbsps ground dill weed
□ 1 tsp salt   □ 1 tsp white pepper
□ 1 tbsp chopped tarragon   □ 12oz sour cream
□ 1 tbsp parsley

Wash the potatoes and cut them into 1-inch cubes. Place in salted water and cook until just tender. Remove from the heat, drain and allow to cool. When the potatoes are cold, toss with the remaining ingredients and serve chilled.

GREGORY MARTIN,
WHITE RABBIT CATERING,
HOOKSETT, NH

*Above: the Sentinel is a pine bridge overlooking The Pool in Franconia Notch,
a deep valley between the Franconia and Kinsman mountain ranges.*

BRACE OF DUCK IN PEARS AND GRAND MARNIER

This dish is perfect for entertaining because it is impressive while being very easy to prepare. Fruit is always the perfect complement for the richness of duck and the mustard, Grand Marnier and honey add extra interest to the sauce. With New Hampshire's abundance of game, this sauce can also be used with wild duck.

PREPARATION TIME: 20 minutes
COOKING TIME: 50 minutes
OVEN TEMPERATURE: 400°F
SERVES: 4

INGREDIENTS

☐ 2 whole duck breasts cut from 6lb ducklings

SAUCE

☐ 2 ripe pears, peeled, cored and seeded   ☐ 1 tsp mustard
☐ 1 cup Grand Marnier   ☐ 1 cup honey

Roast the two duck breasts in a hot oven for about 30 minutes. Meanwhile, prepare the sauce. Purée the pears with the mustard, Grand Marnier and honey. Simmer for about 20 minutes. When the duck has cooked for 30 minutes, drain off the fat, place the duck breasts back in the pan and pour over the sauce. Lower the oven temperature to 400°F and bake for another 20 minutes. Skim any fat from the sauce and pour over the duck to serve.

JAMES HALLER'S KITCHEN,
26 LIBERTY STREET,
SOUTH BERWICK,
MAINE
(FORMERLY OF PORTSMOUTH, NH)

Facing page: a misty afternoon in late fall at Indian Head.
Above: Brace of Duck in Pears and Grand Marnier.

FOUR-LAYERED CHEESECAKE

The chopped almonds and shredded coconut that form the base of this cheesecake make a delightful change from the graham cracker crust found on most cheesecakes. Also, this crust couldn't be simpler. Various flavors in the layers combine beautifully to make a cheesecake that tastes as good as it looks.

PREPARATION TIME: 30 minutes
COOKING TIME: 1 hour 55 minutes
OVEN TEMPERATURE: 425°F reduced to 225°F
MAKES: 1 10-inch cake

INGREDIENTS

□ ½ cup butter, softened
□ ¾ cup each of chopped almonds and shredded coconut

FILLING

□ 3lbs cream cheese   □ 4 eggs
□ ½ cup flour   □ 1 cup confectioners' sugar
□ ½ cup dark bittersweet chocolate, melted   □ ½ cup cognac
□ ½ cup almond paste   □ ½ cup Amaretto
□ ½ cup praline paste   □ ½ cup Frangelico
□ ½ cup white chocolate, melted   □ 2 tbsps vanilla
□ ½ cup rum

Grease the inside of a 10″ springform pan generously with the softened butter. Dust the pan with a mixture of almonds and coconut. Press the mixture against the butter to help it stick. Combine the cream cheese, eggs, flour and confectioners' sugar and beat until well mixed. Divide the mixture into quarters and add to one quarter the melted dark chocolate and the cognac. Pour this mixture into the pan on top of the crust. To the second quarter, add the almond paste and amaretto and mix well. Carefully spread across the first layer. To the third quarter, add the praline paste and Frangelico. Blend again and lightly spread on top of the last layer. To the final quarter, add the melted white chocolate, vanilla and rum. Pour this over the top and carefully spread out. Place in the oven at 425°F for 15 minutes; reduce to 225°F and bake for another hour and 45 minutes. Remove and allow to cool completely before refrigerating. Chill for 24 hours before serving. Decorate the top with chocolate leaves.

JAMES HALLER'S KITCHEN,
26 LIBERTY STREET,
SOUTH BERWICK,
MAINE
(FORMERLY OF PORTSMOUTH, NH)

Facing page: this Four-Layered Cheesecake is an indulgent treat with coffee or for dessert.

SOUR CREAM
APPLE PIE WITH
CINNAMON

This is a pie with a most unusual pastry, tasting of cinnamon, maple and cider. That, and a filling of sour cream, Cheddar cheese and tart apples topped with a spicy sugar mixture which cooks to a caramel, adds up to an incredibly delicious dessert.

PREPARATION TIME: 1 hour
COOKING TIME: 55-60 minutes
OVEN TEMPERATURE: 350°F
MAKES: 1 9 inch pie

─── INGREDIENTS ───
─── CRUST ───

☐ 2⅔ cups flour   ☐ 5 tbsps granulated sugar
☐ ¾ tsp salt   ☐ 1¼ tsp ground cinnamon
☐ 6 tbsps butter, chilled   ☐ 6 tbsps shortening, chilled
☐ 2 tbsps maple spread   ☐ 4-5 tbsps chilled apple cider

Above: as the leaves begin to change color, the thickly forested slopes of New Hampshire become a rich tapestry of green, gold and russet.

──── F I L L I N G ────

- ☐ 5-7 tart apples, unpeeled and cut into ½ inch wedges
- ☐ ½ cup shredded Cheddar cheese   ☐ ⅔ cup sour cream
- ☐ ¼ cup heavy cream   ☐ ½ cup granulated sugar
- ☐ 1 egg, slightly beaten   ☐ ½ tsp salt
- ☐ 1½ tsps vanilla   ☐ 3¼ tsps flour

──── T O P P I N G ────

- ☐ 3 tbsps grated lemon rind   ☐ 3 tbsps brown sugar
- ☐ 3 tbsps granulated sugar   ☐ 1½ tsps ground cinnamon
- ☐ 1 cup chopped walnuts

Place all the ingredients for the pastry except, the apple cider, into the bowl of a food processor fitted with a steel blade and process for several minutes, or until the mixture resembles rolled oats. With motor running, pour in the apple cider until the dough clings to itself and forms a ball. Refrigerate for 1 hour. Roll out the dough between pieces of parchment paper and place in a greased 9″ pie plate. Combine all ingredients for the filling in a large bowl and mix until all the apples are coated. Add the apples to the pastry-lined pie plate and pour over any remaining mixture. Combine all ingredients for the topping and sprinkle over the pie filling. Bake on middle rack of a preheated oven for 55-60 minutes, or until the apples are tender and the filling is bubbling. Serve warm or cool.

GREGORY MARTIN,
WHITE RABBIT CATERING,
HOOKSETT, NH

Above: Sour Cream Apple Pie with Cinnamon.

Flavor of
MAINE

BAKED STUFFED MAINE LOBSTER

Plain or fancy, Maine lobster is superb. This "dressed up" recipe has a luxurious stuffing of crab meat flavored with sherry. Wrapping the lobster in lettuce leaves for cooking keeps it moist and adds extra flavor as well.

PREPARATION TIME: 30 minutes

COOKING TIME: 20-25 minutes

OVEN TEMPERATURE: 450°F

SERVES: 2

INGREDIENTS

☐ 2-3lb Maine lobster   ☐ Lettuce leaves

CRAB MEAT STUFFING

☐ 4 cups Ritz crackers, crushed   ☐ 4 tbsps melted butter
☐ ½ cup cream sherry   ☐ 1 tsp salt
☐ 1½ tsps Worcestershire sauce   ☐ 1 drop red pepper sauce
☐ 1lb Maine crab meat

GARNISH

☐ Lemons   ☐ Parsley
☐ Melted butter

Combine all the crab meat stuffing ingredients. Place the live lobster upside down on a cutting board. With a sharp knife, quickly split the lobster down the middle, being careful not to cut all the way through. Take the large claws off and remove 4-6 of the small legs and set aside. Spread the lobster apart and fill it with the crab meat stuffing. Put the lobster back together and completely cover the outside with lettuce leaves. Place in a preheated oven and cook for 20-25 minutes. If using a convection oven use the shorter cooking time. Remove the lobster from the oven, discard the lettuce leaves and arrange the small legs in an upside down V. Put the lobster under the broiler long enough to brown the stuffing. For best results, boil the claws in salted water while the lobster is cooking. Garnish with a fluted lemon half and parsley. Serve with melted butter.

EXECUTIVE CHEF PETER McLAUGHLIN,
THE LOBSTER POUND RESTAURANT,
LINCOLNVILLE BEACH, ME

Previous pages: Portland Head is Maine's oldest lighthouse, built in 1791 amid some of the state's most spectacular coastal scenery. Facing page: Baked Stuffed Maine Lobster.

MAINE STEAMED
CLAMS

Maine clams are soft-shell clams and are delicious steamed, fried or in chowders. As part of a Maine Shore Dinner, they are often called steamers and are served in great piles alongside lobster and corn on the cob.

PREPARATION TIME: 15 minutes

COOKING TIME: 10 minutes

SERVES: 7-8 clams per person

INGREDIENTS

□ 7-8 medium sized soft-shell clams (steamers) per person
□ ¼ cup water □ 8oz-1lb butter, melted

Place the clams in a medium-sized kettle with the water. Cover and cook on medium heat until the clam juice (referred to in Maine as clam broth) boils up through the clams and all the clams are opened. Discard any that do not open. Serve them hot with melted butter and the clam broth. To eat, remove the tissue from the neck, dip the clam in the broth and then into the butter.

THE LOBSTER POUND RESTAURANT,
LINCOLNVILLE BEACH, ME

Facing page: New England Clam Chowder and Maine Steamed Clams are the kinds of dishes that might be served at the Chowder House in Boothbay Harbor (above).

NEW ENGLAND
CLAM CHOWDER

There are many recipes for clam chowder because it is such a traditional and popular dish in New England. Some recipes include salt pork and some don't, but all are delicious. This one makes use of the prized soft-shell clams for which Maine is justly famous.

PREPARATION TIME: 25 minutes

COOKING TIME: 20-25 minutes

SERVES: 5

INGREDIENTS

□ 3 quarts whole milk □ 5 medium-sized potatoes, cut in ¼-inch cubes
□ 1 medium-sized Bermuda onion □ 6lbs Maine soft-shell clams
□ 1 tbsp clam base □ ½ tsp pepper
□ ½ tsp salt □ 2oz lightly salted butter

Place the potatoes in cold salted water, bring to the boil and cook until tender but not mushy. Drain and set aside. Place the clams in a pot with ¼ cup salted water and cook until the natural clam juice boils up and the shells open. Set the clams aside to cool. Add the butter and onion to the pot and cook until the onions turn transparent. Add the milk and potatoes. Remove the clams from their shells and peel off the membrane. Cut the tip end of the neck off (the black part) and add the clams and their remaining ingredients to the butter and onion. Cook over gentle heat for about 1 hour. Excellent when reheated the next day. Serve with oyster crackers or saltines.

CHEF RICHARD A. McLAUGHLIN,
THE LOBSTER POUND RESTAURANT,
LINCOLNVILLE BEACH, ME

Above: lighthouses are a necessity to guide sailors around Maine's craggy coastline (facing page), scene of countless marine disasters.

WEST BAY ROTARY DOWNEAST CLAMBAKE

This style of cooking traces its origin back to the Indians. A colonist was said to be walking along the shore when he came upon several Indians grouped around a large pile covered with a blanket. Tantalizing clouds of steam seeped from the edges of the blanket, emitting a delightful aroma which the colonist found irresistible. He shouted in delight, tore off his jacket and joined the group to share their feast. Be sure to start preparations for your own feast at least 4 hours before serving.

PREPARATION TIME: 1-2 hours

COOKING TIME: 2 hours

INGREDIENTS

☐ Lobsters ☐ Clams or mussels
☐ Corn-on-the-cob ☐ Clam broth
☐ Melted butter

To prepare the pit, dig a hole in the sand about 1½ feet deep, 6 feet long and 3 feet wide. Fill the pit with wood and build a very hot fire. After about 1 hour, add granite-type rocks. Do not add shale rocks or rocks that hold water; they may explode. Place the rocks evenly over the wood and add coals. Add more wood if necessary, After about 2 hours remove all the burning wood leaving just the coals and rocks. To cook the seafood, place a 1-foot-thick layer of seaweed over the coals. Place the lobsters, clams or mussels and corn in separate burlap bags. Cover the bags with 1 foot more of seaweed. Place a potato on a knitted rope bag and place on top. Cover the entire pile with canvass. Cook for 2 hours. If the potato is cooked, the seafood and corn are done. Heat the clam broth and arrange with the cooked seafood, corn and melted butter.

RICHARD McLAUGHLIN,
THE LOBSTER POUND RESTAURANT,
LINCOLNVILLE BEACH, ME

Facing page: West Bay Rotary Downeast Clambake.

NORTH ATLANTIC SALMON AMANDINE

Salmon, at its best, is said to be the king of fish. Traditionally, salmon was served in New England to celebrate the 4th July, but don't save a fish this good for once a year. Arranging the almond "scales" may seem like a daunting task, but for a special meal the effect is well worth the effort.

PREPARATION TIME: 25 minutes

COOKING TIME: 50 minutes

OVEN TEMPERATURE: 350°F

SERVES: 8

INGREDIENTS

- □ 5-6lb whole dressed salmon

STUFFING

- □ 6 cups crushed Ritz crackers
- □ 5 tbsps melted butter
- □ ¾ cup cream sherry
- □ 2 tsps salt
- □ 2 tsps Worcestershire sauce
- □ 2 drops red pepper sauce
- □ 1½ lbs Maine crab meat

COURT BOUILLON

- □ 4 cups water
- □ 3 celery sticks, diced
- □ 1 quartered onion, stuck with whole cloves

GARNISH

- □ 1lb blanched, sliced almonds
- □ 1 egg white

Remove the backbone from the salmon and combine with the court bouillon ingredients in a saucepan or a fish steamer. Bring to the boil and allow to simmer while preparing the stuffing. Combine all the stuffing ingredients and mix well. Spoon the stuffing into the cavity of the salmon. Rub the fish with melted butter and place in the top of the fish steamer or into a roasting pan. If using a roasting pan, carefully pour the cooled court bouillon over the fish. Cover with foil and steam in the oven for about 50 minutes. Remove the fish from the steamer or roasting pan and peel the skin from one side of the fish from the head to the tail, leaving the head and tail intact. Garnish the side of the fish with the almonds, using egg white to hold them in place, to give the fish a scale effect. Brown under a broiler until golden brown.

EXECUTIVE CHEF PETER McLAUGHLIN,
THE LOBSTER POUND RESTAURANT,
LINCOLNVILLE BEACH, ME

Facing page: North Atlantic Salmon Amandine makes a stunning dinner party dish.

MAINE LOBSTER

SALAD

Lobster salad is a luxury dish and the ultimate elegant salad. It is not a dish to economise on, so serve it lavishly. Traditionally, this salad is made with freshly cooked lobster, allowed to cool but never refrigerated.

PREPARATION TIME: 25 minutes

COOKING TIME: 15 minutes

SERVES: 4

INGREDIENTS

☐ 8 1¼ lb live Maine lobsters   ☐ ½ lb salt
☐ ¾ cup heavy mayonnaise   ☐ 4 large lettuce leaves

Fill a 12 quart stock pot ⅔ full with water. Add ½ lb salt (not a misprint) and bring to a rapid boil. Drop in the live lobsters and cover the pot. When the water begins to boil again, cook the lobsters for 15 minutes. Drain the water and allow the lobsters to cool. When the lobsters are cold, remove the claws and the small legs. Remove the meat with a nut pick. Twist the tail section completely around while holding onto the body. Break the ends off the tail (the flippers) and push the tail meat out. Pull the top strip of the tail meat back and remove the black intestinal tract, if present. The top part of the body shell can be pulled away exposing the tomally (the liver) and the body meat. All parts of the lobster are edible, with the exception of the shell, digestive tract and stomach. Cut the lobster meat into ¾ inch pieces, place in a mixing bowl and add the mayonnaise, stirring to just mix. Serve the lobster meat on crisp lettuce leaves. Garnish with parsley sprigs, if desired, and serve chilled.

EXECUTIVE CHEF PETER McLAUGHLIN,
THE LOBSTER POUND RESTAURANT,
LINCOLNVILLE BEACH, ME

Facing page: Maine Lobster Salad is a delicious way to serve that most famous inhabitant of the state's waters. Above: Biddeford Pool in Saco Bay.

MAINE LOBSTER STEW

This is another and probably the most luxurious of the famous shellfish soup-stews from the East Coast. The dill pickles may seem an unusual choice as an accompaniment, but their piquancy is a perfect foil for the velvety richness of the stew.

PREPARATION TIME: 30 minutes

COOKING TIME: 1 hour

SERVES: 8-10

INGREDIENTS

□ 4 quarts of whole milk   □ ¼ cup heavy cream
□ ¼ cup melted butter   □ 1½ tsps Spanish paprika
□ 3¼ lbs Maine lobster meat (see Lobster Salad recipe for method)
□ Pinch salt

Heat the milk and heavy cream in a double boiler. Do not allow to boil. In a heavy skillet (preferably cast iron), add melted butter and paprika. Heat slowly, mixing the paprika and the butter together to create a red butter sauce. Add the cold Maine lobster and heat slowly, turning the meat until warm, but do not over-heat. Add the warmed lobster meat to the hot milk and heat gently for at least an hour. Add a pinch of salt if necessary. For best results, remove the lobster stew from the heat and refrigerate overnight. Reheat the next day. Serve with oyster crackers, dill pickles and hot rolls.

EXECUTIVE CHEF PETER McLAUGHLIN,
THE LOBSTER POUND RESTAURANT,
LINCOLNVILLE BEACH, ME

Above: a fishing boat moored in the harbor at Stonington, where the fishing industry is enjoying a revival. Facing page: Maine Lobster Stew.

DUCKTRAP RIVER SMOKED PLATTER

Ducktrap River Smoked Fish is flavored with brine, herbs and spices in combination with the savory smoke of northern fruitwoods. The Ducktrap Fish Farm in Lincolnville supplies some of the best smoked fish and seafood in the area.

PREPARATION TIME: 15-20 minutes

SERVES: 4 as an appetizer

─── INGREDIENTS ───

□ 2oz smoked scallops   □ 2oz smoked Maine shrimp
□ 1 peppered mackerel

─── HORSERADISH SAUCE ───

□ 1 cup mayonnaise   □ ¾ cup sour cream
□ 1 tbsps grated horseradish   □ Juice of a ¼ lemon

Arrange smoked fish on a platter. Add saltine crackers and horseradish sauce. Garnish each serving with parsley and serve chilled.

THE LOBSTER POUND RESTAURANT,
LINCOLNVILLE BEACH, ME

Above: Ducktrap River Smoked Platter.

MAINE SCALLOPS
JARDINIERE

Beautifully cut garden vegetables in a cream and white wine sauce give a French flavor to the succulent scallops of the Maine coast. Buy the scallops with their roes, which are a great delicacy and, to preserve their round shape, cut them around the middle, if desired.

PREPARATION TIME: 25 minutes
COOKING TIME: 20 minutes

INGREDIENTS

- □ 1lb sliced scallops
- □ ½ cup mushrooms
- □ ½ cup celery
- □ ½ cup carrots
- □ 2oz shallots, finely chopped
- □ ¼ cup dry white wine
- □ 1 pint heavy cream
- □ Pinch salt and pepper
- □ Small clove garlic, crushed
- □ 2 tbsps olive oil

Cut the celery and carrot into thin julienne strips and blanch for 2 minutes in boiling salted water. Set them aside while heating the olive oil in a sauté pan. Sauté the scallops, mushrooms, shallots and garlic until the shallots are just transparent. Add the white wine and reduce by half over high heat. Add the cream and the remaining ingredients, and simmer until the sauce thickens slightly and becomes creamy. Garnish with parsley and serve over rice.

SOUS CHEF ROBERT KULIKOWSKI,
THE LOBSTER POUND RESTAURANT,
LINCOLNVILLE BEACH, ME

Above: Maine Scallops Jardiniere.

MAINE STRAWBERRY SHORTCAKE

Few desserts say "summer" the way strawberry shortcake does. The biscuits can be baked in advance, and they also freeze very well. Shortcake is versatile as a dessert – serve it informally after a barbecue or arrange stylishly to follow a formal dinner.

PREPARATION TIME: 30 minutes

COOKING TIME: 10-12 minutes

OVEN TEMPERATURE: 450°F

SERVES: 6-8

INGREDIENTS

BUTTERMILK BISCUITS

- ¾ cup plus 2 tbsps all-purpose flour
- ¼ tsp salt
- 1 tsp double acting baking powder
- ½ tsp sugar
- ¼ tsp baking soda
- 2 tbsps butter or margarine
- ¾ cup buttermilk

WHIPPED CREAM

- 4 cups whipping cream
- 1 cup powdered sugar
- 2 tsps pure vanilla extract

STRAWBERRY SAUCE

- 3 quarts strawberries
- ¼ cup granulated sugar

GARNISH

- 1 pint fresh strawberries, hulled

Sift all the dry ingredients for the biscuits into a bowl. Cut in the butter or margarine until the mixture is the size of small peas. Add the buttermilk and lightly mix in. Turn the dough onto a floured surface and knead 10 times. Press out to a circle ¾ inch thick and cut with a floured biscuit cutter. Place on a baking sheet and dot each biscuit with butter. Bake in a preheated oven for 10-12 minutes or until risen and golden brown. Remove to a wire rack to cool.

Whip the cream until slightly thickened. Add the sugar and vanilla and whip until soft peaks form. Chill until ready to use.

To prepare the strawberry sauce, hull all the strawberries and place in a food processor with the granulated sugar. Blend until smooth. Strain if desired. To assemble the dessert, place half a biscuit on a dessert dish, cover with sauce and add a layer of whipped cream. Add the remaining half of the biscuit and top with sauce. Garnish each shortcake with more cream and fresh strawberries.

EXECUTIVE CHEF PETER McLAUGHLIN,
THE LOBSTER POUND RESTAURANT,
LINCOLNVILLE BEACH, ME

Facing page: Maine Strawberry Shortcake makes the best of one of summer's most popular soft fruits.

FRUIT MERINGUE
CHANTILLY

During the 19th century in the United States, individual meringues were very popular and much enjoyed at teatime. Meringues are not difficult to make; just be sure that the whites are beaten to stiff peaks before any sugar is added.

PREPARATION TIME: 30 minutes
COOKING TIME: 1 hour
OVEN TEMPERATURE: 275°F
SERVES: 8-10

Above: Fruit Meringue Chantilly.

INGREDIENTS

- 1½ cups egg whites
- ¾ tsp cream of tartar
- Pinch salt
- 2¼ cups granulated sugar
- 1 kiwi fruit, peeled
- 1 fresh pineapple, peeled and cored
- ¾ cup green seedless grapes
- ½ cup seeded purple grapes
- 3 navel oranges, peeled and segmented
- 1 banana, sliced and dipped in lemon or orange juice
- 3 cups heavy cream, whipped with ¾ cup powdered sugar
- 2 squares German sweet chocolate

Let the egg whites warm to room temperature (1 hour). Beat the egg whites with the cream of tartar and a pinch of salt at a high speed. Once stiff peaks form, gradually beat in the granulated sugar, making sure the meringue mixture is stiff between each addition of sugar. Lightly grease and flour two baking sheets and drop the meringues with a spoon about 1¼ inches apart. Bake in a preheated oven for approximately 1 hour or until crisp. The meringues should stay pale in color. Remove to a wire rack to cool while preparing the fruit.

Cut the fruit into small pieces, leaving ⅓ in larger pieces for garnish. Fold the cut fruit into the whipped cream. Build the meringues in a tree formation using the fruit and cream mixture to hold the meringues together. Garnish with the remaining fruit and sprinkle with grated chocolate.

PATRICIA McLAUGHLIN,
THE LOBSTER POUND RESTAURANT,
LINCOLNVILLE BEACH, ME

Above: looking out over the Penobscot River from the small town of Bucksport situated at its mouth.